Forks in the Road

Forks in the Road

My New Life in America

Heidi Smith

Orchard Books

Orchards Books Trade Paperback Edition

Also by Heidi Smith
After The Bombs – My Berlin
Published under her maiden name
Heidemarie Sieg
ABQPress

Why Add Water When Wine Will Do
Orchards Books

Orchards Books
P.O. Box 1819
Taos New Mexico 87571
www.HeidismithGroup.com

ISBN: 978-0-578-16879-1

To Trent with love and gratitude
for always encouraging me -
"You can do it."

Contents

Introduction

Forks in the Road *is a sequel to* my memoir After The Bombs-My Berlin. *I realize that many readers will not have read it. To them, I offer this summary of my life up to the day I boarded an ocean liner destined for New York.*

◆◆◆

I was born during World War II in Berlin. My father died towards the end of the war and it was up to my widowed mother, I called her Mutti, to raise my sister and me.

We lived on the fourth floor of an apartment building near the rail yard. Rubble was all around us. I remember being cold and hungry after the war, especially during the year when the Russians blockaded all roads into Berlin. The allies' airlift of food and fuel saved us from surrendering to the Soviets. It took well over ten years for supplies, and the economy, to slowly improve.

When I was five years old, my younger sister was in a children's hospital with tuberculosis. I declared then to become a nurse to help children get well.

During high school I realized that I didn't qualify for a free college education because of my average grades. Mutti could not afford the tuition for nursing school. Reluctantly I entered business school instead, a trade school that was free. I graduated after three years, but business did not interest me as a career.

It was a common practice to spend a year abroad after graduation to further educate yourself. The idea grew on me. I couldn't afford to travel, but working in another country would be a start. I always liked working with children. I had a seven-days-a-week afternoon babysitting job since I was twelve until I entered business school to earn some needed money. To find work as a nanny was a logical step.

Many young women were going to England. Because of the many cases of pneumonia I had growing up, Great Britain's climate would not be favorable for me.

Mutti suggested working in France or Switzerland instead. Once I started applying for jobs, I had an offer caring for three children in Basel, Switzerland, within two weeks.

However, when my train arrived in Basel, the family had retained their nanny. I didn't have a job or money for a return ticket. A family friend wanted to hire me as a cook, even though I had never really cooked a meal. The woman offered to teach me and I accepted. That turned out to be a good decision. She was an excellent teacher and I found that I had a talent for cooking and well-honed taste buds!

After more than a year I left for a position as a nanny for three young children. I was in charge of the children but also cooked for the family once they discovered my love of food and cooking skills.

The year flew by; it was time to go back home. I wasn't ready to go back to the retail business though. With my friend Margit, whom I met in Basel, I decided to go to America for a couple of years.

With the help of the family in Basel, we had job guarantees just outside of Manhattan. The consulate in Switzerland granted us green cards in record time. We planned to work and travel - first a year in New York and then move on to San Francisco. We wanted to explore that huge country before going back to Germany.

My memoir ends when we are leaving Germany aboard the ocean liner M.S. Berlin for New York in May of 1963.

My readers have asked, "...and then what happened?"

Here is the rest of my story.

Heidi Smith
Taos, New Mexico
2015

I – The New World

Au pair in New York

As the jagged skyline of New York got closer and closer, my friend Margit and I were very quiet. The M.S. Berlin, the ocean liner that brought us from Bremerhaven to New York, was passing by the Statue of Liberty in the early morning. Loud cheers erupted on all decks.

Many unknowns were ahead. I didn't feel any of the excitement our fellow passengers displayed.

All we knew was that we had jobs. Mr. and Mrs. Guidi, my previous employer in Switzerland, helped secure them for both of us. With that we applied for working visas at the American Consulate in Zurich. Our green cards were issued within a couple of months. Margit was going to be cook and housekeeper for the Bridges family in Briarcliff Manor, a short drive from New York City. I was hired as a nanny by the Bodens, friends of Mr. and Mrs. Guidi. They also lived in Briarcliff with their three children. Mrs. Boden and Mrs. Bridges were going to meet us at the pier.

It was May 24, 1963, a sunny morning and we reveled in the calm after some stormy days while crossing the Atlantic. Curiosity brought us to New York. Our plan was to be working in New York for a year, then hopefully find a job in San Francisco before going back to Germany. Besides working we wanted to learn English and see as much as possible of the States. I knew a bit of English; it was taught from fourth grade through high school. I continued studying the language by taking evening classes at the university in Basel. Margit didn't know any English. She grew up in East Germany where Russian, not English, was the foreign language.

Margit and I met at a women's group in Basel. Miss Muller, a Swiss native, was leading the weekly sessions, an opportunity for foreigners to meet and socialize. Most of us were working as au pairs for a year or two. Working in another country to broaden one's education was encouraged at the time. We were twenty-one, both had graduated from business school and were making a detour before going back to that 9 to 5 life.

Some women traveled and worked in other countries before going back to their hometowns. America was the number one choice. Miss Muller shared letters she received from unhappy girls in New York who were stuck with a family. When a couple paid for the girls' fare to New York, the exchange was a promise to work for them for a year. After we listened to the letters, we discussed how to best manage situations like that. We vowed not to go to America until we could pay the fare ourselves so as not to get trapped in jobs we didn't like.

On this calm, clear morning in the harbor of Manhattan, we watched for hours as passengers left the ship and disappeared into the waiting crowd. "Maybe we should go now," Margit and I turned to each other at the same time, "They'll think we're not on this ship." By now it was 11 a.m. and we slowly made our way down the steep gangplank.

"They" were our new employers, Mrs. Boden and Mrs. Bridges, whom we had never met. We spotted two ladies behind the metal barrier, calling our names "Heidi? Margit?" We made a dash to say hello. They welcomed us to New York with a slight shaking of their heads for taking so long. Finding our suitcases before going through customs was easy because only a few were left in the holding area. Customs was a quick formality with passports and green cards in our hands.

At last our suitcases were stowed in the trunk of Mrs. Bridges' car. The car was exactly like the ones I remembered from movies and photos of America. It was a large, off-white convertible with red interior, and the top was down. I climbed onto the back seat and settled into a very cushy leather seat as Mrs. Bridges pulled out of the almost empty parking lot. I soaked in the scenery as we left Manhattan and approached rural Westchester County.

After a very quick 45 minutes, we arrived at the Bodens' house. I was making quick translations of information between Margit and Mrs. Bridges. Phone numbers were exchanged; Margit or Mrs. Bridges could call me any time for translations.

The Bodens' house was a two-story colonial style home, similar to many in this rural residential area. My room was in the basement, adjacent to the large family room that included a TV. Mrs. Boden showed me around while explaining, "My husband and the children will be home by late afternoon."

The children, between six and eleven years old, arrived by school bus at about 4:30 p.m. Sam, Lisa and Tommy were lively and polite and quickly went outside to play in their extensive yard. Mrs. Boden said, "That's what they like to do every afternoon – just run around."

Mr. Boden worked in the city and unless there was an accident on the highway that would cause a delay, "he arrives on the dot of 5:30 p.m. every day," Mrs. Boden smiled. They were both slim and almost six feet tall. That explained the children's heights, as they were all tall for their age.

Mrs. Bridges called several times that first afternoon. She wanted me to explain many tasks to Margit: about her room; what needed to be done today; what time to have supper ready; the likes and dislikes of her husband; their routines – all were separate phone calls. They were easy conversations because Mrs. Bridges was very patient and Margit a quick learner.

After supper Mr. Boden gave me a ride to Margit's house, less than a mile away, as was prearranged. Later one of the Bridges' sons would drive me back. It was a routine we kept up every evening.

Margit's head was spinning with the new language that was all around her. Nobody knew any German. We went over the day ahead and rehearsed some English. Instead of using a dictionary, Margit made up her own book of words and phrases that would help her get around.

The following day was Saturday. Mrs. Boden drove the children to Little League baseball – the three of them were on different teams, Mr. Boden went to play golf and I stayed behind to clean up after the children.

The children's rooms were a mess with toys and clothes on the floor everywhere. The children's bathroom looked especially bad; soap scum in the shower and sink; toothpaste all over the counter, the large mirror over the counter splattered with soap and toothpaste, all towels on the floor. I had never before seen a mess like this! I peeked into the Boden's room and it only looked slightly better, but I didn't clean that too.

When the children returned, they marveled at their clean rooms and the bathroom. "I expect you to pick up after yourselves at the end of every day." I said and added, "What you drop, you pick up." Sam, Lisa and Tommy looked at me very surprised. They didn't say a word and nodded in unison.

Sundays and Thursdays were our scheduled days off. On Sunday we started on our sightseeing trips. We had a long list of must-sees. We took the early train from Ossining to the city. Grand Central Station and Fifth Avenue were on our agenda.

Fifth Avenue was as grand as we envisioned it, the skyscrapers were overwhelming. We stopped at every store window on Fifth Avenue, all the way to the beginning of Central Park. Margit and I were amazed at the prices, especially for shoes. They were so much lower in price than what we were used to. All stores were open, which was definitely new for us. In Europe every business, except restaurants and bars, closed Saturdays at noon for the weekend.

We loved Manhattan instantly. It was easy to learn the street layout to find our way around. At lunch time we stopped at *Horn & Hardart,* a self- service restaurant that we'd heard about. It was very different from any restaurants we encountered in Germany and Switzerland. We perused the plates that were displayed behind small glass windows, much like soft drink machines today. Sandwiches, salads and desserts on plates in single servings were ready to eat. After dropping coins in the slot next to the window, the window could be opened by turning a knob and the plate removed. We skipped lunch and opted for our first slice of lemon meringue pie and a cup of coffee.

Our heads were spinning from our first adventure in town and we headed back to Westchester in the late afternoon. We watched TV for a while at my house. This would become our usual evening activity - watching a show or movie. Television shows were a natural introduction to our new language. It was conversational English as it was spoken in the U.S., not the formal Oxford English that I'd been used to.

During commercials we made plans for our next time off. The early sixties was a wonderful time to be a tourist in New York. We avoided some questionable areas we'd heard about and felt safe wherever we went. Mrs. Guidi had given me a very good New York City guide book. We had taken turns reading it during our leisure time on the 10-day journey crossing the Atlantic. By now the book was full of check marks at every place we wanted to see and some were marked "maybe if we have time." We decided on Radio City Music Hall for Thursday.

Monday morning was chaotic as the children got ready for school. I stayed nearby as they dressed, changed their mind and tried several different outfits, dropping clothes on the floor as they went. Then a quick breakfast of corn flakes and a piece of toast. They were ready as the school bus approached the house at 7:30. I waved as the bus left and went back into the house.

I hadn't seen either parent so far. Mrs. Boden came into the kitchen to make coffee. I went up to the children's rooms. On the landing to the second floor I met Mr. Boden. He handed me a pair of his shoes, a jar of shoe polish and a brush and said, "Here, this is your job from now on. I'm leaving in a half hour and they need to be ready." He continued down the stairs and disappeared into the kitchen.

Wow! I couldn't believe what I just heard. That's not my job, I'm the nanny! In the different households that I've experienced as an au pair, the man took care of his shoes; not the wife, not the children and not the nanny! I didn't say anything and polished the shoes. This was totally unexpected. I was upset and it was hard to focus. I stood still for a few minutes and calmed myself. "This isn't so bad. I can handle it. Hopefully there isn't anything else coming."

After Mr. Boden drove off to his job in the city, Mrs. Boden met with me in the kitchen. "I'll show you around the house again and point out the things that'll need to be done." She elaborated how the house was built to their specifications and that they moved in just a year ago.

"The parquet floors are not sealed and will need to be stripped of old wax and refinished. It hasn't been done since we moved in." She looked at me. I got the message.

"The windows need washing inside and out." She looked at me. I didn't comment. She continued, "Mrs. Guidi wrote how handy you are with a sewing machine. When all the cleaning is done, I would like you to make curtains for all the windows. I already have the fabric and lining material for them."

I was so upset at what I heard that I clenched my teeth really hard so as not to say anything! I don't know if it showed in my face but my stomach was hurting badly. This family didn't need a nanny; they wanted a cleaning woman. In Europe, every household position is very clearly defined. There are housekeepers, cooks, cleaning women, laundresses, butlers, maids, personal maids and nannies. Everyone knows the duties of each job and does not encroach on others. The Bodens obviously wrapped all positions into one.

I wanted to leave right there and then. I hadn't a clue of where to go or what to do! Thinking of the Guidis, who co-ordinated this job, kept me from making any rash moves. We had a very friendly and respectful relationship and my loyalty to them stifled the urge of running out the front door.

I called Margit. Mrs. Bridges asked if I was all right, "Oh, yes," I said. I unloaded my misery to Margit and we decided to talk again in the evening.

I knew that I could not stay with the Bodens for a whole year under these conditions. I started the job of cleaning the house from top to bottom. I didn't have much contact with the children. Their after-school activities kept them away until dinner time. Mrs. Boden was in charge of all meals. In the following days and weeks I scanned all job advertisements. Opportunities were limited.   As I cleaned I was thinking of different jobs I could possibly apply for. In the evenings when Margit and I got together we tried to come up with a solution for me.

One day Mrs. Boden dropped the hint that she would like me to sew clothes for the children when I was done with the curtains, "just like you did for the Guidi children in Basel," she said. At that point I was still scrubbing down floors and hadn't started on the curtains. I knew I had to leave soon.

What about my green card? Could I leave this job? We didn't have any written contract. This experience now validated the scrimping and extra work to pay for the ship ticket myself. Since I paid for my passage, the Bodens couldn't make me stay, could they?

On our next Thursday off, I went to the German Consulate in Manhattan. I explained my situation and asked specifically what would happen to my status in the U.S. if I left the family. "Nothing," said the clerk. He explained that my green card made me eligible to work anywhere. "As long as you do not become a burden to the U.S. Government you are free to do as you wish."

I was greatly relieved to know that. But I still wrestled with being obligated to the Guidis in Basel for having helped and enabled me to come to the U.S.

Every day, as I tackled another room, I hoped that maybe I could tough it out. But then reality set in. No, I didn't want to live like this for a year, not even for my friendship with the Guidis.

Three weeks after I started on the rooms I was finally done. It was Friday the 21st of June. Saturday, after Mr. Boden arrived home from the golf course, I asked to speak with him. "I did as I was asked, all rooms in the house were thoroughly cleaned," I said and continued, "It is my understanding that I was hired as a nanny, not as a cleaning woman." I told him that the job was not working out for me. I gave two-weeks notice, enough time to get someone else.

"No!" he yelled and stomped his foot. "I want you to leave my house by noon tomorrow!" He continued yelling, "You are like all the others. All you want is to go to Manhattan and party!"

"No," I said. "I didn't have to come to New York to party. I grew up in Berlin and partied all I wanted." I continued, "I was hired as a nanny and that is not what my work here is. I'll leave tomorrow morning as you wish."

"You can't do this! I'll call the authorities first thing Monday morning. You won't be able to get another job. I'll see to it that you get deported."

"I have been to the German Consulate and was told that nothing will happen." I turned and went to my room.

I was kicked out right away. I hadn't thought of that. I figured two weeks' notice would give me time to find something. I called Margit and relayed the entire episode. She said she'd ask Mrs. Bridges if I could stay with her in her large room for a couple of days. Mrs. Bridges called a few minutes later, "You are welcome to stay with us as long as you need. Tom (their son) will pick you up tomorrow at 11 a.m."

It was a great relief. I would be all right for a few days. While I was gathering my things I heard the Bodens arguing in their bedroom, which was above my room. Lots of yelling by him, and she was crying. Stuff was thrown, I heard heavy thumping from furniture falling. I guessed it was Mr. Boden. I knew I made the right decision.

On Sunday morning I didn't see the Bodens or the children. I was waiting in the driveway with my suitcase when Tom drove up. He didn't drive the family car the way he used to do when he was driving Margit or me back and forth. He arrived with the black business limousine.

The family was watching from the living room window. I must say I felt very good as we drove off.

◆◆◆

Doors Open

"All I know is that the family hasn't been able to keep any help for more than a month. I'm sure you did what you had to do," Mrs. Bridges told me after I arrived at their house. It made me feel better.

I planned to find a small apartment and a job in Manhattan. After the experience with the Bodens, I felt discouraged about another nanny position. I saw many ads for retail sales clerks and felt confident about getting work.

Mr. Bridges, president of Harcourt, Brace & World – one of the largest textbook publishing houses in the U.S. - drove to the city every day and gave us a ride Monday morning. During the drive to Manhattan, Margit and I scanned the morning paper for affordable apartments. We found several prospects.

With newspaper in hand we walked to all the apartments we had marked. All were in lower Manhattan, some in scary looking areas; broken glass, windows boarded up and trash everywhere. Finally we found a safer looking neighborhood. A one-bedroom apartment at ground level on 24th Street would do. I made a $50 deposit and could move there in two weeks.

I noticed Help-Wanted signs in shop windows not too far from the apartment and made appointments for interviews the next day.

We met Mr. Bridges at the company's Third Avenue location just in time to hitch a ride home. On the way he asked all about our adventures and we relayed everything, including my pending job interviews.

After supper, Mr. Bridges asked me back into the dining room. He offered me a job as personal chef at his company. "We just added another floor in the building. It'll give us several more offices, a large boardroom and also a full-size kitchen. I'll need a cook to prepare and serve lunch every day for myself and any guests. I know you are an experienced cook. Are you interested?"

I didn't have to think. "Definitely!"

"Good. It means you'll have to live closer to the city, but you have taken care of that already. You can start next Monday." He added, "The kitchen will be ready in two weeks. Until then you can run the Xerox copying machine in the printing room. Is that all right?"

Margit and I did a celebration dance around the kitchen! This crisis was solved. I knew I could do the job. I cooked and served formal lunches and dinners in Basel for over a year. I had many recipes in my arsenal.

On Sunday I packed my suitcase and headed to the city. I was staying at the YWCA until I could move into the apartment. The deposit on the apartment and some other expenses had eaten up most of my cash. I had just enough to get me through the week. Margit would come on Thursday, her payday, and loan me some money until I got my first paycheck.

I didn't know that I had to pay for the room at the Y every day, not when I checked out as I had thought. Counting my cash I realized that I had just enough to pay for my room through Wednesday. There was nothing left for food. I had two rolls of *Life Savers*. I divided the candy into allowances to get me to Thursday afternoon. I figured that I would be hungry, but I was hungry often as a child and knew that it would be all right for a few days.

Monday morning I went to the publishing company. The Xerox machine was at one side of a cavernous printing room. Five large printing presses were busy all day. The operators were all men. They welcomed me warmly and asked many questions about my German background. Then they went to the printing presses and I settled behind the Xerox machine.

Secretaries arrived constantly with copy orders. Some wanted to operate the machine themselves, "The copies have to be perfect, not crooked the way they usually turn out."

"You can leave them with me. They will be just as they should be," I promised. Reluctantly they left their originals with me. When they returned to pick up the copies, they were impressed. Now they trusted me with the job without hesitation. I was the copy queen!

The men in the background chuckled. Of course, it was not complicated to make copies. I also became expert at fixing the machine. This was 1963 and the copier was as big as two large desks and needed constant adjusting. I was busy and the hours went by quickly; it also kept my mind off food.

It was already very hot in New York. Temperatures were in the high 90s with very high humidity. I wasn't used to that at all. The printing room was air conditioned and I was very comfortable during the day. Evenings at the 'Y' were more of a challenge. Trying to stay neat with all this sweating was a lot of work. Everything needed to be washed constantly. The laundry room was busy all the time. I joined the line for a turn at the ironing board early in the morning.

Just before lunchtime on the second day Lori, a German clerk, stopped by. She invited me to join her at lunch in the cafeteria. I did but said, "I already ate," keeping the Life Saver diet to myself.

"Where are you staying?" I told her about the apartment. "You know you can rent a room for a lot less," she said. "The room I rented from a German woman in Queens is still available. I could take you there after work today." It sounded promising. I wouldn't have to spend half my salary on rent.

Lori and I took the bus to Queens. Mrs. Fleischman, an elderly widow, lived in a small two-story building in Astoria on a quiet residential street.

"Betty, please" she said, as we entered her house. The room was small, but it was all I needed. Kitchen privileges were included and I agreed to the rent. Betty and I got along from the minute we met.

I tried to get my down payment for the apartment back from Mr. Klein, the apartment building manager. He was evasive. "I don't tink I can do 'dat. Givin' back a deposit... we don't do 'dat. I have to find anoder tenant. I'll ask de boss. Call back in a week." I heard a low chuckle before hanging up. I wasn't hopeful after his comments. But I really could use the $50, so I made a note to call again.

By Thursday my Life Savers were gone. I drank lots of water to silence my growling stomach and counted the hours until I met Margit. At five o'clock I was waiting in front of the building. Margit should arrive any minute. Third Avenue was at the height of rush hour, jammed with cars and pedestrians. I waited. It was 5:30 and no sign of Margit!

What could have happened? What if she didn't come? I had no money! The Y would put my things into storage. Where could I spend the night? I didn't know anybody in New York! At noon the next day was payday and I had to get through somehow. That was all I could think of – get through somehow. Maybe I could sit in the Y's lobby overnight and if not I, could wait the night out at Grand Central Station. My thoughts were going round and round.

At 6:00 p.m. I started pacing the block from one corner to the other. Traffic started to thin out. Suddenly I heard, "Heidi!" Margit was on the other side of the street! She had been waiting a couple of blocks away and was worried too. She had misunderstood the street address. I was so relieved and quickly crossed the street to meet her.

We laughed as we headed to the Y to pay for another night. Then we went to the German neighborhood on 86th Street for a hearty dinner at *Kleine Konditorei,* one of many European restaurants there. We craved some of our favorites. Margit had *Sauerbraten* and I opted for *Beef Rouladen.* We both also had a large, refreshing glass of German beer.

After work on Friday I headed to Astoria. The temperatures had reached 100 degrees that day and it was oppressive in my tiny room. Betty was going to sleep in the basement where it was much cooler and said, "Why don't you do the same?"

Everything had fallen into place. I felt secure and I slept really well.

◆◆◆

Enjoying the Big Apple

Margit came to town every Thursday and we continued our sightseeing schedule of Manhattan and its surroundings. We started to have a busy social life through my landlady.

Betty, her sister Hedy, their relatives and friends included us in Sunday outings and birthday celebrations. Hedy was widowed also and lived in Manhattan. One of her friends was the owner of The Steuben House Restaurant, a German restaurant on 22nd Street. We often went there to eat, the atmosphere was friendly and the food very good.

The customers were mostly Germans who'd been in the country for at least 30 years. If the weather was not so inviting, we sometimes spent all afternoon at the restaurant, listening to people talking about their experiences. Conversations were easily started and spanned from, "How did you find this place?" to "We come here every Sunday," and often settled into, "I came to New York with my parents when I was two." Growing up German in America often was not a smooth road. "In school everybody knew that I was German and was called Nazi – period!"

Betty and Hedy also introduced us to the customs and celebrations of the German community. During the summer, many clubs had summer fests in the German tradition - German music, folk dances, lots of bratwurst and beer.

In September, the Steuben Parade in Manhattan was a day-long festivity. It celebrated German General Van Steuben. German clubs from all over the states and Germany traveled to this annual celebration.

Steuben was a Prussian military officer who came to the U.S. late in 1777. He is considered the father of the Continental Army by teaching them military skills, tactics and discipline. He wrote a war drill manual that was used for many years. Late in life he was General George Washington's chief of staff. I had never heard of him and his contributions to the U.S. military. I doubt that I would have been aware of all these facts had I not rented the room from Betty.

1960s tourist with proper white gloves

Out of the blue I had a phone call from Bob, a friend from Basel. He was the only American in our ex-pat group. When he heard that we were going to America, he asked for our addresses and said, "I'm going back soon also and will show you New York." I was looking forward to seeing a familiar face.

During dinner at The Lorelei in the German neighborhood he asked me about our New York experiences. He told me that he grew up in New York, "As a matter of fact, I lived just a couple of blocks from here. My father has had his dentist practice here forever." Our conversation was like the lighthearted banter I was used to in Basel.

During dessert Bob said, "Listen, I have an offer for you. Instead of renting the room form Betty, you could move in with me. I really like you. You can cook and clean and we can also sleep together." After a pause he added, "But you need to know that I can never mention you to my parents or take you to meet them. We are Jewish. They don't want to have any contact with Germans."

I stopped eating. "Excuse me," I said and went to the ladies room.

I was furious! I was shaking. This guy, whom I believed to be a friend, was propositioning me to be his maid and mistress, even though I was German. How open-minded of him!

From the ladies room I walked back towards our table. Bob rose to hold the chair for me, but I kept right on walking.

This definitely reinforced my "no thank you" policy towards dating while traveling. Oh sure, Margit and I often went dancing and to a pub for a drink and dinner. But we stuck to our resolve, "We go and leave together." As seemingly unattached women we quickly got the attention of men wherever we went. But we were not interested in dating. We wanted to finish our obligations in New York. Then we planned to work in San Francisco for a year or so before heading back to Germany. But we certainly enjoyed partying and flirting.

After a couple of weeks the kitchen was ready. Mr. Bridges usually had between two and six guests, rarely more. They were mostly writers, sometimes editors and department heads. I knew the day before who and how many guests to expect. I ordered staples from Aristides and all was delivered within the hour. For vegetables and meats I stopped by the store in the morning before getting started in the kitchen.

Among the luncheon guests were writers like William Saroyan, Anne Lindberg, and Günter Grass. The guests often stopped by the kitchen on the way out to thank me. Saroyan especially liked the Veal Blanquette and said, "I haven't had this for quite a while!"

Mr. Bridges had a different opinion, but made it a point of not communicating with me directly. Any comment like, "He doesn't like sauces," or a suggestion, "Don't wear pink! He hates it," came via Margit.

Over time I realized that the business climate was very different from the one I was exposed to in Berlin. Mr. Bartel, president of Wegena in Berlin, where I worked for three years while also going to business school, visited each of the 40 retail outlets throughout the city at least twice a year. All employees knew him. None of my colleagues in the printing room had ever seen Mr. Bridges.

After the kitchen was sparkling again I went to the printing department and took care of the pile of copies to be made. The printing crew always was happy to see me and wanted to know how I was doing.

Especially on Friday mornings Bob, Larry, Carl, Peter and Pat, the printing department's head, gathered around the Xerox station. They wanted to hear about my adventures. They knew that Margit came to town Thursdays and that we were sightseeing. None of them had been to the top of the Empire State building, visited the Statue of Liberty or been on the Staten Island Ferry. I had a rapt audience as I described our excursions in detail.

The printing crew in turn educated me about baseball. Whenever there was a game, the radio was turned up high so that all could listen over the racket of the machines. They explained to me what was going on in the game. "Darn, this was a strike!"

"What's that?"

"A strike is when the hitter misses a ball that was really in......"

Baseball was new to me and all their well-meaning commentary went right over my head.

On the way home I shopped at a grocery store in Astoria for my supper. I couldn't wait to cook without having to worry about who would like it.

As the weeks sped by, I was getting restless. I had to be very careful and manage my budget from week to week. I did not get my $50 apartment deposit back from Mr. Klein. I looked at other job possibilities, but salaries were not much better than what I was earning. The plan of going to San Francisco did not look so appealing any more. I wondered what kind of work I could get. Would I be able to earn enough to travel some more and also save for the return trip to Germany?

I was considering going back to Berlin before our year in New York was up. I didn't really have a plan of what I would do there. Applying for a sales position in a department store was probably where I would start.

Mr. Bridges' personal secretary joined me at lunchtime once a week. She was very friendly and genial. Sometimes she asked me about Germany. One time I mentioned that I was thinking about going back. I had picked an early December departure that would get me to Berlin in time for the Christmas holiday.

A few days before Columbus Day weekend, a week after that conversation, I was called to the human resources office. The elderly woman there said, "We understand that you are preparing to go to Germany in December." I nodded.

"Well, we decided to let you go. We will have to hire another cook. Why wait 'til December when we can do it now."

I was totally taken by surprise and burst into tears. She added, "Your kind is not wanted here. Go back where you came from." I was too shocked to ask what she meant by 'your kind.' I guessed she meant being German. In a daze I took the check with one month severance pay and left.

How naive I was! I should have never mentioned my thoughts of returning to Germany. Obviously, Mr. Bridges' secretary was his eyes and ears in the company. I was mad at myself for being so ignorant. It was a lesson I never forgot.

When I gathered my coat and bag in the printing room, Pat came over and asked why I was crying. "Oh, no! I'm so sorry for you. We won't be hearing any more New York discovery stories." He walked back to his printing machine. A minute later he returned, "Why don't you come back at lunch time tomorrow. We just may have a surprise for you."

A cake and a little wrapped box were sitting on top of the Xerox machine. My buddies gathered around and watched as I opened the box and card beside it. As a group they wished me well for the future and gave me a 'good luck charm' for my bracelet. I was buoyed by the warm feeling that came my way. After a hug from each, we waved and I was on my way home.

I often spent time with Margit in Briarcliff. Whenever I came across Mr. Bridges, he was as friendly as ever. There were no hard feelings on either side. What I experienced as his personal chef, how I was let go, was nothing personal – strictly business.

Where to go from here? I couldn't go to Germany yet, I didn't have enough money for the fare.

Margit and I had already paid for a weekend trip to Washington, D.C. Armed with the *New York Times* we boarded the bus. We didn't see much of the scenery at first because we were scrutinizing all Help-Wanted ads.

What made me most content was cooking and working with children. That's what we were looking for.

I wanted to work with children for as long as I could remember. When I was young I dreamed of being a nurse in a children's hospital. The seed for that was planted when my mother and I visited my sister in a sanitarium for children with TB in 1946. I wanted to help children get well. That dream came to a stop when there were no funds for college. I went to business school instead. After graduating I still wanted to work with children. The idea to work as a nanny was very appealing. That's how I arrived in Switzerland in 1960.

A family needing a governess for their three young children jumped out of all that small print. Perfect. "I'll call them when we get back," I promised myself.

We were approaching Washington quickly. It was so different from New York City. No skyscrapers. The avenues were wide and sunshine was reaching every nook. It gave us a new picture of the United States - not all cities were like Manhattan.

The bus dropped us off at The Mall. From the Lincoln Memorial to the Capitol we saw every spot within walking distance. The Kennedy White House with its grandiose rooms was definitely a memorable highlight. It was the site with the longest lines. Luckily, bus tours didn't have to wait. We were ushered into the building quickly and there the pace slowed. All tourists moved slowly through the rooms. It was giving us ample time to observe the decor furnishings, some dating back to other presidencies.

The bus also stopped at the Washington Cathedral, not as impressive as St. Patrick's Cathedral in New York, which we had seen the week before. Our tour continued on across the Potomac to Arlington Cemetery. The top of the cemetery opened to a wonderful panoramic view of the city. It was a peaceful spot.

Our trip also included a boat ride on the Potomac River to Mt. Vernon. Gliding down the river was like being in another country. Mt. Vernon offered a glimpse into the country life of centuries ago. Walking through the house, gardens, root cellars and barns, I imagined what that daily routine must have been like - much more complicated without the conveniences we take for granted today.

Back in New York after the holiday, I waited until 9 a.m. before calling the number in the paper. I was hoping that the position was still available. Taking care of three young children - that was exactly what I wanted to do!

"Yes, the position is still open," said the voice at the other end of the phone. I made an appointment for an interview Thursday afternoon.

◆◆◆

Nanny in Manhattan

Armed with references from my nanny positions in Basel, I headed to upper Fifth Avenue. Mrs. Arnum asked about my experience and I translated my Swiss references.

We walked through the spacious apartment. Mrs. Arnum showed me the tiny maid's bedroom and bath, passed the kitchen in the back of the apartment.

I was also introduced to the children. The Arnum children were three- months-old Sandy, Hannah - almost two - and Bobby, a mature four year old. All were similar to the ages of the Guidi's children in Basel. I felt that this could be a good position for me. I certainly liked the idea of being across from Central Park.

Mrs. Arnum called the next morning to tell me I had the job. Thursday afternoons and most Sundays would be my time off, which was customary for household staff. The salary included room and board. The money would go a long way since I had no expenses. Finally I would even be able to save.

I gave Betty a week's notice and commuted from Astoria the first week.

Sunday was moving day with Margit's help. Carrying my suitcase and several boxes, we changed busses a couple of times and finally arrived at my new home on Fifth Avenue. I thought the address was pretty cool!

Mr. Arnum was a busy attorney; his wife was involved with several non-profit charities. We established a comfortable routine. I was in charge of the children, including cooking all their meals. Four-year-old Bobby just started kindergarten; Hannah was going to have her second birthday soon; Sandy, the baby, had a sunny disposition. Hannah and Sandy were easy to entertain with books and singing in the morning. After Sandy's nap we all headed to a playground in Central Park for the afternoon. If it rained we played games in the family room. Some afternoons Mrs. Arnum was joining the children. Mr. Arnum often kept the children company while we were having dinner. Once the children were in bed, the evening was mine.

I was content, and life was looking better again. A return to Berlin was still in the back of my mind.

Then a letter from my sister Margot arrived. "You should not come back after just a few months in New York. All the money you spent will have been wasted!" No word of understanding that I was homesick. I was extremely ticked off at the lack of empathy. I didn't write back.

My sister's letter was a wake-up call. As usual, my sister had taken charge, overriding whatever Mutti (my mother) might want to say. Mutti usually went along with whatever Margot decreed to have peace in the house. It was a reminder that in Berlin my sister would continue to tell me what to do. I admitted to myself that I wasn't ready for that routine just yet. I resolved to forget about going back to Berlin and to look ahead to the year with the Arnums and then move on to San Francisco as planned.

I continued watching television in the evenings, expanding my grip on English. While I was renting the room from Betty I learned how important immersion in a new language is. German-born Betty had been in America for close to 40 years. She was a stay-at-home mom. Her relatives and circle of friends were German. Her two sons spoke perfect English, but her conversation was a heavy mix of German and English words and grammar.

Margit and I felt we needed to speak English whenever we could, or our learning would be minimal. We had already resolved to converse in German as little as possible when an incident on a city bus reinforced that decision. Two women were sitting in front of us, speaking loudly in German. They criticized everyone on the bus; the awful color dress one woman was wearing; the fat stomach hanging over a man's belt; one woman's wild hairdo that made her look like a hooker. The women obviously felt secure in their language, believing no one could understand them. They would have been embarrassed had they known that a couple of Germans were in the next row. When the bus reached our stop, we turned and said, "Auf Wiedersehen" as we exited.

We didn't want to be caught like that. Even if it was difficult for Margit, because of her limited vocabulary, we resolved to speak only English in public.

One a Friday in November, Mrs. Arnum came to my room while I had my afternoon break. What could be the matter? She never came to my room. "The President has been shot in Dallas. I turned on the TV. Do you want to come and watch with me?"

I followed her quickly to the family room. The usual soap opera was not showing. Instead, shortly after we got into the room, Walter Cronkite of CBS announced, "From Dallas, Texas, the flash – apparently official - The president died at 1 p.m. Central Standard time, 2 p.m. Eastern Standard time, some 38 minutes ago."

Oh no! How could this be? This is the United States! This went round and round in my mind.

John F. Kennedy, hero to all Berliners, was dead? When the Wall was built between East and West Berlin, it was President Kennedy who assured everyone in West Berlin that the United States would keep the Soviets from taking over all of Berlin. In a show of strength, U.S. Army troops marched from West Germany through East Germany into Berlin. It reminded the Soviets of the allies's presence in West Berlin and Berliners had faith in that support. And just this summer, Kennedy visited Berlin and proclaimed, "Ich bin ein Berliner!" as thousands cheered.

It didn't want to sink in that he was assassinated in his own country. I guess I was naive in thinking that this couldn't happen here.

The Arnums usually didn't watch any television, but we were glued to the TV constantly, never leaving the room together. One always stayed in case any news was forthcoming. I did my daily routine with the children, played games and went to the playground. Coming back to the apartment my first question was, "Any news?"

Two days later, a Sunday, we were watching the apprehended gunman, Lee Harvey Oswald, leaving Dallas Police Headquarters. He was being escorted to a car that was going to take him to the Dallas County Jail. Suddenly a man stepped out of the small crowd, raised one arm and aimed a gun towards Oswald. He was shot and died instantly.

We were speechless. Did we really see this? What else could possibly happen? Is this country going mad?

We also took turns going to church. It seemed the only action we could do. Only a few people walked along the streets on Sunday afternoon, usually a bustling time of day. The church was filled.

The funeral was televised on Monday. The Arnums and I watched it together. It seemed like a bad dream to me when it was over. It was good that we could talk about it all, and that I didn't have to digest this shocking event alone.

On our days off, we continued to explore Manhattan. We usually met at Grand Central Station and went sightseeing from there. If we didn't have any plans for the evening, we continued on to the German neighborhood on 86th Street and its restaurants. Almost all waiters were Germans and we enjoyed exchanging experiences with them. We took turns between *Café Hindenburg, Kleine Konditorei* and *Die Lorelei.* Sometimes we skipped dinner and ordered dessert instead. A slice of chocolate layer cake or apple strudel satisfied us for the evening.

The Arnums and the Bridges, as well as employers of our friends, were season ticket holders at many theaters and the Metropolitan Opera. We gladly took their tickets when they couldn't go themselves. I relished occupying a choice seat at the old Metropolitan Opera house. I think we bought tickets to the theater only once during the time we were there.

Sundays we either met at my place or I took the train to visit Margit in Briarcliff. We often ended the day cooking. The families spent the evening eating out and we had free reign of the kitchen.

When we cooked in the Arnum's kitchen in New York, the aroma brought Mr. Arnum around, "Hmm, what's cooking today?" Once it was *Szegediner Goulash* – pork and sauerkraut. He sampled right from the pots. Mrs. Arnum asked for the recipe. She needed something that would travel well in a dish for reheating. The Arnums went on several ski trips to their house in Vermont. She could ski all day and just reheat the goulash for company.

Mr. Arnum loved to eat. We talked about food with him whenever we met. He always had suggestions for restaurants not to be missed. With his pointers we had enjoyed wonderful meals in Chinatown and Greenwich Village.

The Arnums asked if we'd like to cook for a few formal dinner parties they would like to host at their apartment. Of course we were delighted. The children stayed with their grandmother when Margit and I were chefs.

The New York World's Fair opened in April 1964. The exhibits spread over a large area in Flushing, an area in Queens, and was easily reached by subway. It was the biggest fair I had ever seen.

Many countries showed the best they had to offer, including their traditional foods. It was impossible to see everything in one or two visits. Margit and I went there several Thursdays in a row. The U.S. exhibits focused mostly on developing technology. Computers were still new and huge, often filling almost a whole room. We saw small computers that could be put on a desk at the fair.

Most memorable was what they called the Picturephone. We lined up at the Bell Pavilion for a chance to see the touted technology up close and give it a try. We could see the person at the other end of the line on a small screen. I remember thinking, "What if I just put my hair in curlers?" Today, of course, I love Skype and Facetime!

Most of the fairground is a tennis complex now where the U.S. Open is held every year.

In the summer both our employers escaped the city heat and humidity. The Bridges family and Margit left Westchester County to spend a month in the Thousand Islands region near Montreal.

The Arnums spent July on Cape Cod. They were driving to the Cape with two children. I was taking the oldest, Sandy, by plane to Hyannis. It was my first airplane trip, as well as Sandy's. Because I had the young boy to look after, I didn't have time to be nervous. Sandy was excited about going by plane and I just followed his lead.

The family had a large house and guest cottage at a small bay near Hyannis. The children and I stayed at the guest cottage. We were less than 100 yards from the water and went to the beach every day. I also took the children for walks in the nearby woods. To their delight we found wild raspberries and blueberries. It became one of our favorite daily routines.

I spent as much time as possible on the beach. I had been to the ocean only once before on a short holiday on the coast of Spain. I loved it.

I discovered the large library in the main house. That collection included all of Ian Fleming's 007 spy novels. I read at least a book a day, mostly at night and in my free time on the beach. *On Her Majesty's Secret Service* was, and is, my favorite. The sun didn't bother me and I found that I tanned easily.

During this time Margit had a week's vacation and came to stay with me. I arranged for two days off to spend in Boston. We knew we wouldn't be back and wanted to see everything. We walked every step of the Freedom Trail, in our customary high heels, of course. Then on to Faneuil Hall. That was more like the markets we'd known in Germany. We joined many tourists in 'family style' dining at Durgin Park, a landmark eatery since 1827. It was crowded and noisy and the food servings were generous.

Harvard, across the river in Cambridge, was next on our list. We found out how large the campus was while trying to find the Fogg Art Museum. Our guidebook mentioned their art collection. We also saw an amazing array of large gemstones.

On Mr. Arnum's recommendation we had dinner at Locke Ober, "best restaurant in Boston," he told us. We were not disappointed. I had a superb creamy veal dish.

In August, Mr. Arnum drove everyone in the station wagon to their house near the Sugarbush Ski Area in Waitsfield, Vermont, where we would be for the month. I was in the back entertaining the children.

In the morning we went for walks, finding blackberries on low hanging branches. Afternoons were spent at the Sugarbush Inn's large swimming pool. Many families with small children enjoyed pool time when the sun was shining. Sandy learned to swim by himself in the deep end. He also got brave enough to jump off the low diving board.

Many New Yorkers had vacation homes in Vermont. One day, just before my day off, Mrs. Arnum had a call from another woman with a German nanny. Ruth Henderson, Mrs. Skitch Henderson, asked, "Do you think we could get those two girls together?" She emphasized that her nanny did not speak much English and some company, especially German, would be good for her. So, Mrs. Arnum drove me to the Henderson's house near Sugarbush.

Out of the front door walked their nanny Sigrid. I knew her! We both worked together at a clothing store in Berlin, but didn't stay in touch. What a surprise for both of us! We marveled at this chance meeting and spent our free days together.

On one of our days off, Sigrid and I went horseback riding at a stable near the Sugarbush Inn on the mountain road. Peter, our riding instructor, gave us novices minimal 'how-to' directions and led the way into the hills.

Before we even got around the first bend, my horse headed towards an apple tree. He continued into the low hanging fruit laden branches. I bent back to avoid a branch, but it was lower than I thought and was swept out of the saddle. Within seconds I was sitting in the grass. No harm done. Peter chuckled and advised, "Get back up on the horse, so he knows that you're not scared." I did, and the remainder of our ride was uneventful.

Peter invited us for a drink at the Sugarbush Inn bar afterwards. Some of his friends were lounging in the bar. "Hey, Bill, Trent and George," Peter said, "here are Sigrid and Heidi, two visitors from New York. We just had a nice ride through the backwoods." Then, to my embarrassment, Peter immediately described my falling off the horse. Everyone had a good laugh and after a bit of small talk, they went back to their conversations.

While in Vermont, Mr. Arnum suggested the idea of being a ski bum for the winter. He knew my passion for skiing. Before coming to New York I learned to ski in the Swiss Alps and was eager to continue.

I didn't have any idea what ski bum meant. Mr. Arnum explained, "This would be ideal for you. You work part-time in exchange for room and board and a season pass, and you get to ski every day." The idea of skiing everyday was very appealing. It thought you had to live in the Alps to do that.

My year with the Arnums would be over in October. Mrs. Arnum said, "You can certainly stay with us until December when the ski season starts." It sounded tailor-made for me, but Margit and I were supposed to go to San Francisco.

I called Margit. She told me, "Mrs. Bridges has helped me with a job in San Francisco already. It'll be easy to find my way around. I'll be fine." All right. All I had to do was get a job.

On one of my hitchhiking trips to Sigrid's house I met Trodd Fortna, ski instructor and lodge owner. He told me about Judy Bragdon, who was going to open a day care center and was hiring. She planned a center, next to one of the ski slopes, where skiers could leave their small children for the day. This was a unique idea at the time - her slopeside nursery became the first in this country.

Trodd said, "You can work there for half a day and in the evening you can be bartender at my new lodge. The Golden Horse will be finished in December."

By the time I was back in New York, I had a job at Judy's *Valley Day School,* where I would be sharing a bunk room and get a season pass. Tips for bartending at *The Golden Horse* would yield some cash. I was all set for the coming winter.

◆◆◆

II – Vermont

Ski Bum in Vermont

In 1964, skiing was not yet a widely practiced sport in the United States. Most businesses in ski areas barely survived as the season was usually short. Businesses would hire ski bums, give them room and board and a season pass. Ski bums worked sometime during the day or evening and skied when they had free time.

The ski area sold season passes to business owners at a great discount rate. Employers rented houses to accommodate their ski bums. *The Sugarbush Inn,* for example, had a separate building, *The Annex*, for their staff. Others rented bunk beds in dorms for the entire season. If a business, a restaurant for example, had to hire regular employees with salaries, many would have folded early.

After Thanksgiving, I took a train from New York to Vermont and headed for the *Sugarbush Ski Area* near Warren. Being a ski bum was a good trade-off for me. All I needed was a roof over my head and a season pass. My jobs at *The Valley Day School* and *The Golden Horse Lodge* assured me of both.

The ski area had just completed its latest project - *Sugarbush Village.* It was a development at the base of the ski trails, similar to a mountain resort in Vail, Colorado. A covered bridge led visitors from the parking lot to the village, its shops, restaurants and condominium buildings. *The Valley Day School*, called The School for short, was in the center of the village.

The School was a slope-side day care center where parents could drop off their children and then head to the trails for the day. Besides being a day care center, Judy Bragdon, the owner, also taught first through sixth grade. Local children were enrolled for classes and skied in the afternoon. It was the first type of mountain day care center in the U.S. We were busy whether there was snow or not.

A back room at the school turned into a bedroom that I shared with Joan, another ski bum working at the school. Joan was on her college break. Her classes would resume at the end of January. Most ski bums were college students, and some were taking an entire semester off. A few were from Canada.

In early December, the necessary staff and ski bums for all businesses were in the valley, a nickname for the Sugarbush area. Now we needed snow to get the season started. Weeks passed and all we would get was a dusting of snow, not enough for skiing. We needed some good fresh snow. (Snowmaking was still in the future.)

This waiting time was ample opportunity to get to know each other. Every evening we headed to The Blue Tooth, the most popular bar in the area. The music was loud. Beer was on tap, served generously by Tiny, a popular, over-sized bartender. It seemed as though the entire valley was congregating there. From the owners of Sugarbush, Sarah and Damon Gadd, to Frank the dishwasher at one of the lodges, everyone stopped by 'The Tooth.' All talk was about skiing, or the lack of it.

Close to Christmas it happened. It started snowing. Just in time for the holidays, the ski season got under way. When the slopes were finally snow-covered, Stein Erikson, the new ski school director, also arrived. Everyone was very excited to meet the World and Olympic champion!

A welcome dinner was held at the Golden Horse Lodge. Although the lodge had not officially opened for business, the chef produced a fitting dinner for invited guests. Sally, the lodge's breakfast server, and I were waiting on the illustrious crowd. It was fun to eavesdrop between courses; it was ski talk.

Trodd and Lixie Fortna, owners of the lodge, had been valley residents for many years. Besides having several businesses, Trodd was a ski instructor in the winter. He was a very good skier and loved to tell skiing stories with a heavy European accent - although he was American. He probably picked up the accent from Lixie, who emigrated from Czechoslovakia as a young woman.

Lixie was the comptroller at the ski area. She was a generous and caring woman with a quick smile. Lixie took one look at my designer ski outfit and laughed, "That will never do here. You'll freeze on the mountain." I had memories of spring skiing in Switzerland and no clue about the winter weather in Vermont. "Here," she said, "I get free stuff all the time from the clothing reps coming to the area." Lixie handed me a maroon windproof parka and matching stretch pants. Along with a black fur hat, the parka kept me warm on the slopes all winter. The fur hat was actually much warmer than the standard knitted caps, which most skiers wore.

Warm and fashionable

Trodd and Lixie's daughter, Rosie, was training every day in hopes of making the U.S. ski team. We saw her running up and down the mountain road and schussing straight down under the lifts when there was sufficient snow. Rosie made the ski team and competed in the 1968 Winter Olympics in Grenoble, France.

During the Olympics, huge crowds gathered at *The Golden Horse* to watch all the skiing events on television. Whenever there was a glimpse of Rosie, we yelled and cheered. She did not medal, but we were as proud as if we were her parents.

Once the ski season got under way, I worked at The School in the afternoons and was bartending at *The Golden Horse* afterwards. Mornings were free for skiing. Joan, working at the French bistro *Chez Henri*, had the same schedule. We both headed to the mountain early every morning to be on the first lift at 8:30.

Chez Henri, run by Henri and Rosie Borel, was below the school. *The Inside Edge,* The Edge for short, with American fare, was across the narrow street. The restaurant and bar had its grand opening when the ski season got underway. Two brothers, Rick and Trent Smith, were the owners. Rick, short for Eric, was running the downstairs bar and lounge; Trent was in charge of the street-level restaurant.

I remembered meeting Trent briefly at The Sap Bucket, the cozy *Sugarbush Inn* bar, when I was in Vermont during the summer. When we met again he recalled, "You were the one who fell off the horse."

I liked him immediately. He was very handsome and friendly. I felt as if I knew him. When Trent looked at me, it felt like sunshine coming my way. I really wanted to get to know him. I asked Joan, "Trent seems like a neat guy. Do you know anything about him?"

"Yeah, he is. I've heard he recently got engaged."

It hurt to hear that. I was so disappointed, but spoken-for guys were off-limits for me.

Joan and I regularly went to the bar at The Edge after we finished work, before heading to our room across the street. The bar was also the place where the ski instructors spent their evenings. Most of them were Norwegians, like Stein, a few were from Italy, Germany and Austria. Dale, Chip, Frank and Easty were the lone Americans. That's how it was in those early years of skiing, the instructors were mostly sought-after Europeans. All were good friends throughout the season.

The ski instructors were part of our 60s ski bum fraternity. It also included many locals who were either skiers or had jobs at the ski area. The community was so small that I saw everyone at least twice daily, usually at lunchtime at the Gate House, the base lodge, on one of the many trails and again in the evening while partying.

Stein Erikson brought both athleticism and elegance to skiing in the valley. He was known for having created a back flip on skis. This aerial stunt was the beginning of free-style skiing. It revolutionized the industry. Once the season was underway, Stein showed off the Flip every Sunday after lunch to the assembled crowds at the base of the mountain. It was not something we tried to copy, but we admired the flip.

Everyone, however, tried to emulate the elegant carving turns that Stein also was known for. During the week few visitors where skiing. Ski weeks were not part of the business yet. Week-ends were the only busy times. So, on week days the instructors had very few classes to teach. They usually invited us to ski along with them. The instructors were copying the 'Stein turn' and patiently tried relaying the technique to us. Whenever there was open terrain I was practicing to rotate my hips extreme enough to be able to hold a long carving turn. It felt great when it worked! Watching a long line of skiers, sometimes with Stein heading the group, winding their way down a hill in long, sweeping turns, was a beautiful sight.

At the beginning of the New Year, I suddenly came down with a high fever. Dr. Quimby, the local general practitioner, made a house call. He diagnosed pneumonia and said, "You better go to a hospital. The mountain just is not a good climate for recuperating." Joan drove me to Heaton Hospital in Montpelier, 40 miles away. Luckily I had Blue Cross and Blue Shield insurance to cover the expenses.

During my brief stay there, many of the hospital staff stopped by my semi-private room that I had to myself. Apparently the valley was in the news. Several people had been arrested for dealing cocaine. Did I know about heroin use in the valley? Did I know any of those people?

Cocaine use was still relatively unknown to the general public and they were shocked. I knew the people who were arrested, but shook my head, "No, I'm not familiar with them."

I was not that shocked. I remembered reading about a fifteen-year-old girl overdosing on heroin and dying in a public restroom in the 1950s in Berlin. It made a lasting impression. I never tried any kind of drugs, not even pot. I kept my vices to beer, the occasional scotch or bourbon and cigarettes.

I knew the musician and his wife who were arrested in the valley, and was surprised. I had no idea that cocaine was making the rounds. I was aware that people were users, but not that cocaine was their choice of drug. At one of the usual after-hours parties, I noticed a famous model, often visiting for the weekend, sitting stone-faced on a chair. "What is the matter with her?" I asked.

"She's stoned," was the reply. I thought it was booze, but later realized it was some sort of drug. I never saw any other evidence of drug use.

Joan's parents invited me to stay with them for a few days to get my strength back. When I returned to the valley, I was told that I lost both jobs. Business was slow.

Trodd, the owner of *The Golden Horse*, started bartending himself. Judy told me, "Birgit, her only employee, and I can handle the small group alone. You can stay in the room if you can find another job."

As far as I knew all jobs were taken in the valley. I headed to The Edge, across the street, looking for sympathy. Rick and Trent listened to my tale of woe. Their ski bum employees were male according to their motto, "To keep life simple, no females will be hired." Both promised, "We'll ask around."

The following evening, Trent said, "We need another waiter in the restaurant. Against our rules, you can have the job if you want it. Do you have any experience?"

I didn't. But I knew all about table settings and serving. As a personal chef in Manhattan, I cooked and also served many guests. "I can handle waitressing," I promised and started the next day.

It turned out to be a wonderful job!

During the week many locals came to this new steak-house-type restaurant. The atmosphere was "New England rustic." Lunch was served on placemat settings, but for dinner it was white tablecloths and dark red napkins. Bruce, their established ski bum waiter, and I managed all the tables on weekdays.

On Fridays and Saturdays the dining room was packed with out-of-town visitors. Bruce and I were joined by Harvey and Eddie, the week-end ski bums. Eddie was strictly a waiter. Harvey was waiting on tables, as well as being the expert on wines. Tips were most generous. I could really save now. After the season I planned to join Margit in San Francisco as planned.

After dinner the downstairs bar was in full swing. On week-ends and holidays it turned into a night club with live music. Jazz was the favored style. Vocalists, trios and groups from New York, as well as local performers, played at The Edge. Alan Eager and Art Blakey were some of the better known appearing artists.

George and Rick were the bartenders, Sam was the bar waiter. The crowds kept them busy.

There were more men than women in our 'fraternity.' Dates were plenty to choose from. Trent stayed on my mind. I liked him more than ever. During the past months I had plenty of time to observe him. He had a great sense of humor and didn't make a play for every female coming his way. That sure was different from most men, whether single engaged or married! I noticed that Trent's supposed fiancée was never around. I didn't want to ask any questions. Joan kept her ears open and also could not locate this mystery woman. Trent never came to any of the after-hour parties.

There was nothing to do after-hours but go to parties. Bars closed at eleven or midnight and then a group usually moved on to someone's house. Sometimes we would even go to another house if we knew there was a party going on. It was always the same crowd, with visitors sprinkled in on weekends. Sally, Joan and I went together. Joan had a car, but we also walked great distances from house to house. As the hours passed, there was lots of proposing and sweet-talking coming our way. Pairs moved home earlier than the singles. But the three of us usually left parties together.

I remember one time Sally and I had a weird proposition. We often chatted with a couple, probably in their forties – we thought they were old! We never saw them skiing, but only at the bars and parties. They seemed nice enough, often talking about their mail-order business.

At one of the parties they invited us to their house for another nightcap. Shortly after the first sips of my bourbon they mentioned, "We really like this house. It is so close to everything. It also has a sauna. Want to see it?"

As we walked downstairs into the cellar, the conversation turned to sex. "Especially after a sauna session, sex with three or four people can be quite something."

Sally and I looked at each other. "We better go. It's getting really late, and we have to get up early," I said. We turned and raced upstairs.

"It's ok. I'll drive you home," he shouted.

"No, thanks. We can walk." And that we did. By moonlight we walked over a mile along the narrow snow-covered road. "Is that why they are so friendly to everyone, looking for multiple sex partners?" We were both wondering. It was the first time I'd heard of it. I guess that fit right into the 'everything goes' attitude that existed in the ski world community.

We didn't listen to the radio, read newspapers or watch television. I didn't know anyone who had access to television. Whatever happened around the world between December of 1964 and March 1965 was off my radar. All days centered around the weather, skiing and partying at the mountain area. It was the most carefree time in my life.

Ski conditions were not always great. Below zero temperatures, combined with the heavy eastern snow, regularly turned the slopes to hard ice. I skied in all conditions and weather. It was unthinkable not to head to the slopes. Before getting on a lift, I often headed to the ski shop to have the edges of my skis sharpened. Sharp edges were a must to negotiate the hard, icy patches. When it was raining or there were too many bare spots limiting the runs that were open, I opted out.

On those days, ski bums gathered at the Gate House, the base lodge. We spent the day playing chess or poker. Then everybody headed off to work and met again at parties after.

Until March, the winter months went by without any variation of our routines. March brought spring skiing. The warmer temperatures kept the snow pliable for many skiing hours. I skied all day and usually just made it to my 4:30 p.m. starting time at The Edge.

Those were also the days when Bruce often called in sick. He'd say "I drank too much after lunch and can't work." Bruce was not the only one. Everybody reveled in the mild weather and great skiing. Beer was the liquid of choice at lunch and was freely imbibed. And then they continued skiing. I didn't dare because I didn't want to risk crashing and not being able to work.

The season was winding down. Business was really slow during the week and we were waiting for weekend skiers. The after-hours party crowd was growing. Even the business owners joined because there was nothing else going on. Some of the parties were farewell events for those who could not stay until the ski area closed.

To my surprise, I saw Trent at one of the parties. He was by himself and I went to sit next to him. "Nice to see you here," I said. "Wanna talk?"

Trent and I were talking nonstop. By one o'clock in the morning, he was hungry and we went back to the restaurant. In the kitchen I perused the fridge and started to make turkey and tomato sandwiches. "Do you cook?" he asked.

"A little."

Eventually I asked him about the rumored fiancée. "There's nobody," was the answer.

My heart started pounding, but I was hoping it wouldn't show. Trent and I started dating.

♦♦♦

The Future Is US

———————•—•———————

I was in love and Trent made it clear that he felt that we belonged together. From the day we became a couple, we talked about having children. But he did not react whenever I broached the subject as the end of the ski season loomed. He did not give me any indication that he wanted to see me after I left.

With previous boyfriends, I had changed my plans to stay in the relationship. They didn't go anywhere. I remembered a talk my sister and I had with my widowed mother, long ago. At the time we were determined to find a husband for her. "We may be better off if I have a husband, maybe not. Don't believe that a man is the answer to everything," she said.

I often remembered her words. Observing other relationships and marriages, getting married was not high on my wish list. It was different with Trent. I really envisioned life with him. But I was determined not to hang around. If it was not to be that I had a future with Trent, I might as well leave now.

The job as stewardess with Pan Am, that was supposed to start in May, was canceled due to new height requirements. At 5'1", I no longer qualified. So I decided to continue with the original plan of my stay in the United States. After the ski area closed, I planned go to San Francisco to join Margit who was already working there.

We would work and travel for another year before heading back to Germany.

Ginny Oliver, who had worked in the slope-side ski shop, invited me to stay with her family in Manhattan. In mid-April, when the season ended, I packed up and went to New York with Ginny. Trent also headed to New York for his annual monthly duty in the Naval Air Reserves at famous Floyd Bennett Field.

I signed on with a nanny service to tide me over until I secured a job in San Francisco. I was working every day in homes all over Manhattan.

Trent called and we made a date for his first evening off. We went to Frey's Pub, Trent's favorite New York hangout. At the end of that date he asked the question I was hoping for. I didn't play any coy, waiting games. I said "Yes, of course!"

"I don't have any money to buy a ring," he said.

"Don't worry," I murmured, "a ring is really not important to me. You can always buy one later." Trent was quite relieved.

As Trent recalled later to our children, "I realized Heidi meant it when she said she was going to San Francisco. When we went to dinner in New York, I thought I better not let get her away. Outside Ginny's apartment that night I told her that we should get married."

Both of us couldn't get the smiles off our faces. After a couple more kisses, Trent quickly left to get back to the base on time. I was walking on air when I entered the apartment. Ginny and her parents were still in the den. I said, "Trent asked me to marry him. Isn't it great?!!!"

"It's about time. I wondered if it was actually going to happen," Ginny said.

A Most Memorable Day

The Inside Edge was closed until the 4th of July weekend. We set the wedding date for the weekend before, June 27, at the Waitsfield Congregational Church, with a reception following at the restaurant.

There was not much time to plan the wedding, but we managed to send invitations to friends and family. For days I was going from store to store in Manhattan searching for a wedding dress. Everything was too frilly for my taste. Finally I found a simple white sheath at Sak's Fifth Avenue. After that, everything fell into place.

During our preparations, I realized that I was pregnant. We were both still in New York and at our next date I told Trent, "I'm going to have a baby."

"Really?!" He was grinning from ear to ear.

"Yes!" I cautiously continued, "You know that changes things a little. We don't have to go through with the wedding if you don't want to." I didn't want Trent to feel that he now had to marry me. I knew many single mothers in Germany and figured that I also could manage.

"Don't be silly. Of course, we'll get married. We talked about having children right away from the beginning." That sealed it. I was happily pregnant but we kept it to ourselves.

Trent's mother, Nancy, arrived a few days before the wedding. We had a congenial get-to-know dinner at *Gallagher's*, a favorite bar and restaurant. His grandparents and several aunts and uncles came the day before and stayed at *The Sugarbush Inn*. I was happy to meet some of Trent's extended family.

After a luncheon at the Inn, Big Tom, Trent's very jolly grandfather, walked with me through the clothing store and gift shop. "Pick out anything you like. It'll be my treat." I never had such a generous offer. I couldn't think of anything I wanted or needed. "Thank you so much, but I have everything I could possibly want."

Big Tom was surprised, "I've never heard of such a thing or have known anybody like you!"

Years later I realized that I should have picked something so that he could have had the joy of giving. But I always was in an economy mode - don't buy something if there is no need.

Our wedding day, a Sunday, was a perfectly beautiful summer day. It was warm, but not too hot, with no threat of rain.

None of my family could come from Germany. I arranged to call and talk with my mother at our neighbor's phone an hour before the 3:30 p.m. wedding. Mutti wished us well and promised to visit as soon as she could manage. I remember being very cheerful because I knew she was sad for missing the wedding. I missed having her with me. But I also knew that it would have been difficult. She didn't speak any English and would have been lost when we went on our honeymoon.

I would have loved for Margit to be at our wedding. She was still working in San Francisco and it was too far to come for the weekend. But she visited us in the fall when she was on her way back to Germany. She met Trent and gave her stamp of approval, "I'm glad you found each other."

The wedding ceremony was a simple affair. Ginny was Maid of Honor, our friend Mike Rocchio walked me down the aisle. Eric, Trent's younger brother, was Best Man.

Our friend Harvey took over in the restaurant's kitchen. With friends and Trent's relatives helping, he produced a beautiful reception supper. Lobster salad was the star of the buffet. Tiny, the bartender, busied himself behind the bar. Chip and Bruce, among other friends, pitched in serving drinks.

Before the reception, Harvey was in action early. He picked wild roses and daisies in the countryside and piled them in his top-down Land Rover. Harvey, with Top Hat, chilled champagne and the decorated Land Rover was waiting for us outside the church. Then, to beat the other cars, he took a shortcut from the mountain road to Sugarbush Village. He said, "Keep your fingers crossed that we don't get stuck," and drove over Sugarbush's leach field to the restaurant.

Family and dressed-up ski bum friends filled the restaurant to capacity. Malcolm Reiss, who was an excellent skier as well as a photographer, recorded all on film. Those photos refresh our memories every time we look at them.

We left the reception around 7 p.m. for our short honeymoon in Mont Tremblant, Quebec. On the way, we got stuck in weekend traffic on Montreal's Champlain Bridge. That was not in our plan. It was long past midnight when we finally got off the bridge. We decided to stop at a motel and continue in the morning. We arrived at our destination later in the morning and thoroughly enjoyed a few carefree days.

On Thursday we headed back to Sugarbush to ready the restaurant for the opening weekend.

A New Family

At first we lived in a two-bedroom apartment over the restaurant that Trent shared with Bill Scheid. After a month we rented a small one-bedroom house in Waitsfield. We bought a washing machine, a black and white TV and a King size bed with a payment plan at Sears. Our other furnishings were mostly Coca Cola boxes and cushions on the floor. Trent's wooden Boy Scout box turned into the perfect cocktail table.

I couldn't really tell that I was pregnant except for my quickly ballooning stomach. None of the pregnancy ills like morning sickness ever materialized.

We realized that a bigger house may be more practical and found a partially furnished one next to the post office in Warren. It was perfect. A large kitchen, dining room and living room were on the ground floor. Three bedrooms were upstairs. We would be using two bedrooms and contemplated renting out the third.

Right at that time our friend Rachel returned from her summer job at the White Grass dude ranch in Wyoming and was looking for a room for the winter. She moved in with us right away.

The three of us fell into a comfortable routine. Rachel arrived home from her ski school manager's job shortly after Trent left for the restaurant. I cooked dinner for Rachel and me. She did the dishes afterward and we settled in for the evening if she didn't go out again.

The baby was due the middle of January. All I had to do was wait.

In the early morning of January 16, Trent and I made our way to Heaton Hospital in Montpelier in the middle of a snowstorm. Due to road conditions, the drive that usually took thirty minutes took over an hour. Heaton Hospital is on a hill. Trent's '52 green Chevy couldn't make it to the top twice. Contractions became more frequent and I was getting nervous. I said "Ok, I better walk."

"Wait, I'm gonna give it another try." Trent was determined, backed way up a long way, put the gas pedal down to the floor and charged up the hill. He made it!

The passenger door hadn't been working for a while, so I quickly squeezed my stomach by the steering wheel and we walked into the hospital. Jason was born a few hours later. We were very proud parents. It's what we both wanted – we were a family.

◆◆◆

Always Have Plenty of Dessert

In the early summer of 1966, we were renting a two-story house next to the post office in Warren. Jason was born in January.

The Inside Edge, the restaurant that Trent and Eric created at the Sugarbush ski resort, went out of business in April. They both had to admit that it took more than a ski season to survive as a business. Sugarbush was not a four-season resort yet. Finances were tight for our family of three.

Trent had an offer to manage a restaurant on Martha's Vineyard. But together we decided not to move. The restaurant business does not jell very well with family life. Trent said, "I'm gone most of the day when Jason is awake and come home when he's asleep. I'll have to look for any kind job for now and figure out what to do next later."

My part-time job was the evening shift at the Toll Shop, Sugarbush Inn's clothing and gift shop. Trent arrived home at 5 p.m. and my job started at 6. Jason was ready for bed when Trent took over. "Remember to check his diaper," I usually said as I was heading out the door.

Trent and I had just settled into our summer routine when our friend Rachel called. "I just talked with Jackie Rose. Ski Club 10 needs a manager and cook. They weren't happy with their French chef!"

She continued, "I told her about your marvelous dishes. Trent could do the managing."

Then she said, "Hans Estin from the club will call you shortly....I just wanted to give you a heads-up."

The call came just a few minutes later. "Hello Heidi, this is Hans Estin. I'm told we need to meet. I'm driving back to Boston later this afternoon. Can you and Trent come to the club today?"

I had heard of the club, but did not pay much attention. Ski Club 10 was formed by wealthy skiers from New York and Boston. They owned a small building near the slopes that was a restaurant "for members only."

"That sounds like it could work," Trent said after I hung up. "Let's go and meet him." With Jason in the back seat of our blue VW bug, we headed up the mountain road, a 20-minute drive.

Hans greeted us like old friends. "I remember you from the Inside Edge," he said to Trent. "I'm very glad to meet you, Heidi. From what I've been told, you are what the club needs this winter, a good cook."

The dining room's walls and wooden floor were very dark. Tables and chairs, covered with dust, were stacked in a corner. It looked gloomy and uninviting. But the almost floor-to-ceiling windows facing the ski slopes let in a lot of light. I could imagine that in December, when the area was covered with snow, the incoming light would be very bright.

Hans walked with us through the restaurant. The kitchen and bar area were at one end of the dining room next to the entrance. The basement held a large room where children of members would eat and an apartment meant for the manager.

We settled at the bar and Hans gave us an overview of the business mechanics. Club 10 was to be open for lunch from 11a.m. to 2 p.m. Saturdays and Sundays from Thanksgiving through Easter, and every day during school vacations. He told us that they also served two dinners through the ski season; one in late December and the other in February. "Normally you'll get between 30 and 50 members and their guests at lunch time. During holidays you can expect 75 to 100. We usually are around 150 at the dinners."

Wow! Except for cooking a large batch of Black Forest potato soup for the restaurant when the chef was sick, I hadn't prepared food for more than 20. This was going to be a new challenge and needed careful preparations.

"May I see the kitchen again?" I wanted to take a closer look to memorize the set up. The area was actually two rooms; one with the refrigerator, professional stove and oven, sinks and dishwasher. Next to it was a smaller room with counter space, a second fridge and shelves stacked with large pots and pans and food-storage containers

As I poked around, we were talking food. "We always have a soup and salad for those just wanting a quick lunch and then head back to the slopes. There also needs to be a main dish for members wanting a larger, more leisurely meal."

"What is your budget for food?" I asked.

"There's none. Just make it good. We have members with exquisite tastes." I loved to hear that – no budget to worry about!

"Oh," he added, "and always have plenty of desserts!"

Trent would be greeter and manager. "You'll see everyone as they come in and start a tab for them, Trent." He continued, "Renato, the bartender, will be writing down all drinks." No cash was needed. Members signed their tabs and would be billed by Hans.

The pay was generous, a year's salary for four months active work. We accepted the job and sealed it with a hand shake.

On the drive home we were both happy and looking ahead to the winter season. "This will be a good job for us. You get to do what you love - cooking. Managing will be pretty straight forward," Trent said. The apartment at the club was ours, so we could rent it out since we had our house. We could use that money to hire a sitter for Jason.

Everything fell into place. We found Karen, a high school girl from a large farming family in Warren, to be Jason's babysitter. I felt sure that Jason would be well taken care of.

The apartment at the club was rented to our friend Holly.

My head was spinning with ideas for lunches and dinners. The following months I spent planning and writing and rewriting menus. I searched for recipes that would multiply well in my collection of cook books. Soups were easy to plan; recipes are easy to cook in large batches and they keep well.

Main dishes needed to look appetizing and keep their taste while being kept warm. Recipes like poulet flambé, lamb curry and veal blanquette would do well.

Logistics and timing went round and round in my head. I didn't know how long it took for 10 gallons of water to come to a boil, or how long for five cups of rice to finish cooking. I took several large pots home and practiced. I scheduled food preparation down to the minute. I gave myself a 15-minute buffer time.

I mapped out a weekly schedule. Wednesdays we cleaned to get ready for the weekend ahead. Thursdays I shopped. On Fridays I cooked the two soups for the weekend. I also baked pies and cakes and prepped as much as possible for the next day. The main dish and salads were left for Saturday mornings.

We took Jason with us everywhere. He was very quiet and happily observing what we were doing. I kept my job at the Troll Shop until the ski season. If Trent came home later than planned, I took Jason with me to the shop. Jason was not yet walking. I carried him into the shop in his car seat and kept him near the cash register desk. Trent then picked him up when he could and went home.

One evening Paul Newman walked in. He and his son were in the area for soaring at the Warren airport. They were looking for warmer clothes than they had brought. Paul noticed Jason and said, "He's a good baby, isn't he!" I was tongue tied and could only smile and nod. I was a proud and happy mom.

We hired Evelyn, a high school senior, to help in the kitchen. First she served lunch to members' children in the basement. Afterwards she helped with dishes and general clean up. She was a wonderful asset; I could focus on the food.

Trent and I started cleaning the building, mostly on weekends when he didn't work. On Saturday after Thanksgiving we were ready. The great room was spotless. Small tables with freshly polished wooden tops filled the dining area. Classical music was in the air and sunshine streamed through the windows. Savory and sweet aromas from the kitchen permeated the entire building. I was nervous. I wanted to get that first weekend behind me. Then I would really know how my planning worked.

Almost all members came that first weekend. They included investment bankers from Boston; CBS television executives; the New York Tishman family who was rumored to own half of Manhattan; Jackie Kennedy's fashion designers Oleg Cassini and his brother Igor; conductor Skitch Henderson; New York restaurateurs Armando Orsini and Vincent Sardi. Buddy Bombard, a hot air balloon pioneer, was there. Many people from the valley, like our friends Bob and Jackie Rose, were also members.

Food was served buffet style. People could graze all they wanted. I refilled dishes as food disappeared and kept prepping salad in the kitchen. Salad was the part of the buffet that I replenished more often to be fresh and appetizing at all times. Trent let me know when refills were needed, "More soup - it's going fast!"

I was the soup queen, serving each recipe only twice during the season. The same held for main dishes. Recipes were not repeated often.

Members were pleased. Many visited the kitchen, "The chicken was delicious. What makes it so tender?"

"Brandy," I answered and we had a good laugh.

Vincent Sardi made a point to always leave with a compliment, "That was really good, Heidi. I'm not a fan of curry, but this lamb dish was so creamy - I had seconds."

After lunch quite a few members did not venture to the slopes again. They stayed in the great room and played *Backgammon* for hours and hours. Often they downed more drinks than food for the day, leaving the club happy indeed.

Hans was smiling. Members enjoyed their ski weekends and that was the purpose of the club.

Desserts were especially popular. Members often had second helpings of cheesecake. Morv Liebowitz from New York loved the almond cake. He regularly came in again while we were already cleaning up and asked, "Any leftover cake around?"

I learned quickly to cook more food than needed and always had plenty of desserts.

◆◆◆

Almond Cake

Almond cake can be dressed up by spreading a thin coat of chocolate glaze over the top, letting any excess drip decoratively over the sides.
I like the simple version, dusted with powdered sugar, best.

1 cup almonds, skin on, ground
1 cup unsalted butter
1 cup sugar
¼ cup flour, plus flour for dusting the pan
6 egg whites
¼ tsp vanilla
Powdered sugar for dusting

Preheat oven to 375⁰F.
Coat a spring form pan with butter and dust with flour.
Melt butter - just barely – in a large mixing bowl, add sugar and stir until creamy. First add almonds and blend. Then one egg white at a time, fluffing them as you incorporate them. Finally blend in vanilla and then mix in the flour.
Pour into the prepared pan and bake about 45 minutes.
Cool completely – dust with powdered sugar.

16 servings

The Old Vermont Farmhouse

There is no more fitting word than *old* for the house we bought in 1968. Built in 1855, every square foot showed its age.

Trent had heard that we could buy a house through the Farmers Home Administration – FHA - with a low interest loan. Our financial outlook was limited. Neither of us had a trust fund, like many of our friends, nor the prospect of a large inheritance.

Trent's parents were divorced; his father's fortunes had always been like a rollercoaster. His mother Nancy's family, the Waltons, had deep roots in Philadelphia. One if his ancestors, George Walton, signed the Declaration of Independence. Nancy grew up surrounded by nannies, butlers, footmen, cooks and gardeners, on a 41-acre estate in St. David's, Pennsylvania. Her parents' and grandparents' homes, two large exquisite Italian-style stone villas, were nearly side-by-side on the property. The estate included tennis courts, woods, lakes and streams and a log cabin.

The Walton Company, founded before the Civil War, was one of the largest leather tanneries in the world when it was sold to Swift & Company. Taxes started to be a burden. In 1952 the estate was sold to Eastern Baptist College. Trent's great-grandfather created a trust for the grandchildren in early 1900, when 50 years was the average life expectancy. The trustee never changed any of the original investments; the trust shrunk, especially after the crash of 1929 and the following turbulent financial aftermath. The trust was eventually disbursed in the 1980s. It was shared between Nancy, her seven siblings and 40 cousins.

My father's thriving business was destroyed during the war. He died during the fall of Berlin in 1945. My mother, my sister and I inherited what was left of an apartment building after a bombing. Our apartment was one of eight in the old house. The outdated building was in constant need of repair and a burden on our meager finances.

It was clear that our financial health was completely up to us. An FHA loan was likely the only way we would be able to buy a house. We started looking. Our family was growing, Jason was a little over two and we were expecting our second child in September.

Having our own home was especially important to Trent. Until I left Germany, I spent childhood and beyond in one place, the apartment in Berlin.

Trent's family, on the other hand, moved from house to house in Pennsylvania, New Jersey and New York state. His father was busy establishing his own business. By the time Trent graduated from high school, his family had lived in 17 different homes, in six towns and school districts.

"I don't want our children to have that experience. We'll stay right here," Trent often said. When the restaurant closed, he had an offer to manage a restaurant on Martha's Vineyard. He passed up this and other offers for that reason. He didn't want to uproot our family.

He also didn't want to be an absentee father by going to Martha's Vineyard alone and coming home occasionally. For years his father was home only on week-ends. Trent, his brothers and sister dreaded his father being home and doling out punishments. Trent hated it.

Our house hunting left us more hopeless than hopeful. Everything in Waitsfield or Warren, close to the ski area, either was not within our budget or in unlivable condition. We needed a house that we could live in while remodeling. Trent had part-time construction jobs for several summer seasons and would be able to do many improvements himself.

That spring, Trent worked part-time for Steve Flemr, a friend and gentleman farmer, while studying for his insurance and real estate licenses. One of the farmhands told Trent that his family wanted to move to West Virginia and their home in Moretown was for sale. Trent called me, "I may have found a place. We can see it after work." We put off dinner and drove to look at the house.

Moretown was seven miles north of Waitsfield. The ski area had not affected property prices there yet. In Moretown we turned off the main highway. After two miles on a windy, uphill dirt road, we turned onto a smaller country road. Tucked into the hillside, we saw a white house in the distance. It was the only house on the road. We liked what we saw.

Pine Hill 1968

The entire west facing hillside used to be a thriving farm. Open meadows had since been planted with pine tree saplings, now two feet high. The one acre surrounding the house was open, except for assorted crumbling outbuildings and a sagging barn. We turned into the short uphill driveway. One side looking like a junkyard: two station wagons, a refrigerator, and a stove were among the miscellaneous metal junk. This was depressing. But once we were standing in the driveway, the expansive view of the Green Mountains, with Sugarbush and Stowe ski areas in the distance made us forget the junk.

The two-story Cape Cod-style house and attached barn were in various states of solidness. The green tar paper covered roof on the house had straight lines and so did the house. The barn didn't look so good; the upper beam was badly sagging.

Like most houses in Vermont, we entered through the back door. Vernon and Jerry Delong, the owners, had ten children. The oldest, John, who told Trent about the house, was 18. All lived at home. Three official bedrooms were upstairs; two additional bedrooms, the bath, the open living room and kitchen area were downstairs. To accommodate all children, even the walk-in closets had been converted to bedrooms.

Trent and I felt at home right away. We looked at each other nodding and smiling throughout the tour of the house when the Delongs weren't looking our way. We loved the ambiance only old houses have. It felt right and we could imagine the possibilities. The Delongs were pleased that we agreed to the full asking price of $10,000. Trent's mother loaned us the down payment of $500. The FHA loan would take care of the balance. Vernon promised to have all the outside junk removed before the closing.

We were excited about moving into our first home by the end of May. The Delongs were eagerly looking forward to leaving for West Virginia where Vernon already had a job.

The house needed renovating. Not much had been done in a hundred years; ceiling, walls and floors were covered up with various materials. We knew that behind plywood covered walls and vinyl flooring were hand-hewn ceiling beams and hardwood floors, waiting to be uncovered. We figured we could handle it.

Our friends were surprised. "Where are you moving to? Moretown?" They made it sound as though we were moving to Alaska. As far as we could tell, we were the only family from our circle of friends moving there. Today, Moretown is a sought-after town, still rural, more affordable than other towns and the district high school is located there!

I started to pack everything, except what we needed on a daily basis, in boxes. All baby items were packed first. Jason's clothes and favorite cars and trucks would be last. Other toys and all winter clothing disappeared in boxes. The end of May couldn't arrive soon enough for me. I was looking forward to being settled in by early September, the baby's due date.

Trent and I were constantly going over remodeling scenarios. "Jason gets the bedroom in the back. It looks pretty solid. We'll take down that flowered wallpaper later. First, I'll redo the baby's room. Stripping the walls, sheet rocking and painting are not big jobs. It'll be ready when we bring the baby home," Trent assured me.

In mid-May, the FHA notified us that they were out of funds, hoping to receive more from Washington soon. They estimated it would be a month or so. "Don't worry. This happens every year. You're first in line once money is available."

The Delongs were fine with moving the closing to the end of June. June passed without FHA funds. Well, the end of July then. July didn't work out either. The FHA agent felt sure that their promised funds would be in by mid- August. "You'll be able to close by the end of August, I'm certain," the agent assured us.

In mid-July, the Delongs had an auction of all their goods on the property. They were moving by the end of August, closing or not. We kept in close contact with them, relaying any information we were getting from the FHA.

By now I was eight months pregnant and just wanted to get moving over with. The FHA agent called on August 12. "The money is ready for distribution. You can schedule your closing," he said.

Trent hung up. "I'm afraid to get excited. It is actually happening. They have the money!" He called Anna Whiteside, our real estate agent. "Let's have the closing quickly before something else comes up." Anna called back within a few minutes. "The attorney was just waiting for the go-ahead. The closing is tomorrow at 11 a.m." Trent was glad that he could call the Delongs with good news for a change. "Finally we can pack up. See you tomorrow!" Vernon said. Trent thanked him, as we had many times before, for sticking with us until the funds came through.

The moving countdown was on. Packed boxes were stacked in every room with empty ones waiting for the final packing. One week later our friends rallied. Harvey loaded our household goods onto his small pick-up truck. Rachel piled boxes into her VW. Our VW bug was loaded to the ceiling with perishables and Jason's clothes and toys. The caravan headed to Moretown.

While we unloaded, Jason immediately took his cars and trucks and built roads in the driveway.

Unpacking did not take long. We had enough hand-me-down furniture to fill the living room: a sofa, two easy chairs and a wooden rocking chair. A thick maple board resting on cinder blocks became our temporary coffee table. A threadbare oriental rug from Trent's favorite grandmother covered almost all of the bright green linoleum tiles like wall-to-wall carpeting. The blue plastic curtains the Delongs left came down and were replaced with brown and beige patterned, lined ones that Rachel acquired somewhere. The living room looked cozy; we were home. We christened our new home Pine Hill. The old-house-remodeling adventure could begin.

◆◆◆

The Two-Year Plan

We figured it would take two years to renovate the old farmhouse. "No problem," Trent confirmed. Instead of a long to-do list, it is simpler to state what the house didn't need right away: a roof, windows and exterior paint.

One of the first fix-its was buying a huge chain to stabilize the attached barn. Trent attached the chain to the support beams to keep the roof from crashing in and possibly tearing down some of the house.

The first inkling that our plan may need adjusting appeared three weeks after moving in. It was the first frosty morning of September. I had come home from the hospital the day before with our new baby daughter Andrea. Jason was with Trent's mother and would come home later that day.

"We'll be warm in no time," Trent said and headed for the basement. He threw a couple of logs into the metal furnace. Several ducts were going from the furnace to openings in the floor above, the first floor with our living room, kitchen, bath, storage room and one bedroom. On that level the openings had fancy wrought iron grates that let the warm air rise into the rooms. The second floor also had an opening in every room, again covered with a fancy grate allowing the rising heat in.

On this morning, however, smoke oozed out of the furnace and all of the grates and quickly filled the rooms. The metal furnace had cracked at several seams; it was inoperable.

Instead of going to the office as planned, Trent called Rachel and we drove to her house where I spent the day with the baby.

Trent scrambled to buy and install a wood stove in the living room. He also called a heating company for an estimate. "We can get to you at the end of November," they said and Trent agreed. We had the wood stove to heat the house until then. We had planned to get by with the wood furnace until the following year. The FHA gave us a home improvement loan, which was enough to also cover new insulation for the house.

The day before Thanksgiving the oil/hot water system was installed on both floors. Now we had a new oil tank and an electric furnace in the basement.

The insulation was blown into the walls from the outside the following Monday. It is a common procedure with old houses. Holes are cut through the siding where a hose could blow insulation in. When this area was filled, the hole was plugged. Having the workmen around the house was great entertainment for Jason. He watched every move they made and later reported all to Trent. Now our home was warm around the clock. We kept the wood stove to supplement the high cost of oil. It also made the house toasty during frequent power outages.

While we counted the days until the heating system would be installed we investigated the house more. Trent climbed the narrow pull-down stairs to the attic. "I found the windows, come on up and look" he yelled. Fifteen sets of original windows, with 6 over 6 panes were stacked along one wall. Vernon Delong had taken them out. "The house was plenty warm and just the storm windows were enough. They're around somewhere," he told us when we were thinking of buying the house. We were happy to have found the windows.

We also saw the real reason Vernon took out the window. They needed work. Trent counted 180 glass panes; 60 of those were either missing or cracked. The remaining panes were original to the late 1800s. The glass was uneven, had small bubbles and some showed color hues from yellow and blue to purple. We carried the windows into the storeroom where Trent went to work adding new panes where needed. That's what he was doing for a couple of weeks after coming home from the office. Finding the right window for each set took a little doing. The windows definitely enhanced the old farmhouse atmosphere; they kept the rooms warmer too.

The basement had an uneven dirt floor, clearing about five feet. In addition to the furnace it also had a metal barrel holding our water supply. A gravity-fed lead water pipe was filling it. The water was coming from a small brook in the hillside above the house. Trent found the screen-covered intake of the pipe buried in a pool of the brook and knew that eventually we would have to drill a well.

A pump supplied the kitchen and bathroom on demand. Water was also pumped into a newly installed hot water heater. Over the course of the winter Trent replaced the barrel with a tiled storage cistern with larger capacity. When the new furnace was installed, we discovered a fieldstone floor while scraping away dirt to make a level surface. We started filling bucket after bucket with the dirt and carried masses out of the basement. Eventually it added 12 inches to the ceiling height and Trent no longer had to stoop.

The original fieldstone foundation had been haphazardly stabilized with cement. There were two large openings where wood for the furnace had been thrown in. Trent covered the openings with plywood and insulation to keep the cool air out until he could close the gap permanently.

In the spring, we found out why there was what looked like a narrow stone covered stream bed going from one foundation wall to the far end of another.

One morning Trent went to the basement. Within seconds I heard, "Oh, no!" I couldn't imagine what happened and ran to the door. The basement was filled with water to the first tread of the stairs. The spring thaw from the entire hillside behind the house seemed to go through the basement. We knew the ground outside was soaked, but had no idea that the water was filtering through the fieldstone wall into the basement and exiting under the south foundation wall. The exit was clogged and water had no place to go. Now we also knew how the dirt accumulated on the floor.

Trent quickly installed a sump pump to keep the water from reaching the hot water heater and oil furnace. He found the clog and the water receded. Behind the house he was digging ditches to divert some of the water. Throughout the summer he was building berms and installing drain pipes to send water around both sides of the house in the future.

Our bedroom was on the second floor, as well as a room each for Jason and Andrea. Andrea's was the first Trent remodeled. He tore out the papered walls with Jason as helper, and put up sheet rock. When it was done, I painted everything pale yellow and the woodwork white. Then we moved Andrea from the extra bedroom downstairs to the second floor. Finally, we were all on the same floor at night. Jason's room, where the walls were covered with light blue paper featuring ornate flowers, was going to be next.

Bath and kitchen were workable for now. Originally, the old farmhouses had no fancy kitchens with running water and such. In the summer, cooking was done outside in the adjacent summer kitchen (now just an empty shell). In the winter, they cooked on top of a wood stove in the cooking room.

The Delongs set up a kitchen in a corner of the dining room, the former cooking room. Janice Delong was six feet tall; kitchen counter, stove and sink were at a height just right for her. Being 5'1" I used a wooden Coca Cola box to make those levels work for me. I pushed the box from sink to stove to counter as needed. It would be just for a year, right?

Shortly after moving in, Trent bought a motorcycle for his hobby and passion for racing. We made a deal: I could spend the same amount on the kitchen – my passion - when the time came.

Updating the electrical box was one of the first improvements. If I turned on the electric oven, we had to unplug all but one light and the refrigerator or all fuses would blow. The house had the original wiring, installed in the early 1940s. Once the electrical system was complying with current codes, we could use the upright freezer waiting in the barn. It gave me much needed storage between weekly grocery shopping trips.

At the time, the popular TV sitcom "Green Acres" provided weekly comic relief. The show starred Eddie Albert as Oliver and Eva Gabor as Lisa. They played city slickers who moved into an old house way out in the country. Episodes were similar to life at our Pine Hill, except that Trent was handier than Oliver and unlike Lisa, I didn't wear cocktail dresses or evening gowns on a daily basis!

We planned to make a new kitchen and renovate the living room at the same time. The Delongs had installed paneling on the walls and linoleum tile covered the floor. Behind the kitchen/living room area was another bedroom. It became the laundry and storage room until we could renovate; then it would be our kitchen and dining area.

Another baby, Derek in 1970, delayed any remodeling. We were also busy with tearing down several barns, stabilizing the one attached to the house and getting involved with school activities.

Six years later the promised kitchen, where I could move around with ease, became reality. We designed a U-shaped kitchen with dining area close to the adjoining living room. Every item on my wish list was checked off: three walls covered with dark cherry cabinets above and below; a white Formica counter; a double wall oven, one a convection oven; a white four-burner gas cook top; a white ceramic double sink; a dishwasher and the backsplash covered with Italian tile. A new picture window opened to a view of the apple orchard. Plywood flooring would have to do until later. That was all right by me.

Trent was a busy real estate agent by now. Infrequent paychecks were an occupational hazard. It slowed down our two-year plan. We often had to borrow money to tide us over until the next closing. Sometimes several closings happened at once. Then we could pay all our bills and had more money left for another improvement on the house.

We bought an additional five acres, making it a total of six surrounding the house. The remainder of the hillside was still owned by Howard Munn, a well-known area land wheeler-dealer. One day he stopped Trent in the orchard. "Want you to know that I'll be loggin' the upper ridge. Trucks will be going over your water line that's coming down the hill. No guaranteein' that the pipe won't be crushed. Just so I told ya."

We figured he put us on notice, and wanted us to get the pipe out of the brook. Whenever he was selling the acreage along the hill, he'd rather not have it encumbered with our water rights. We could not put off drilling a well. Sure, we could let it run its course and sue him if he broke our pipe. But who wants to do that?

This unexpected project would set us back, but fortune was on our side. Our closest neighbor, Henry Lewis, across the road was in the process of building a house near the hunting cabin he had owned for years. He was planning to move here and drill a well. If the well proved sufficient, we could tap into it. It was. Trent dug a ditch, buried the water pipe that would supply our home from then on.

In the late 1970s, Trent tore a small piece off the pale yellow particle board on the living room ceiling to get an idea of what was being covered. He saw hand hewn beams that supported the second floor. One weekend we took all the furniture out of the living room, covered the kitchen with a tarp and tore off the ceiling. Now the cross beams and wooden planks above were exposed. We painted the brown wall paneling and the window woodwork a cream color. More would be done later, but for now we had a charming living room befitting the old farmhouse.

At that time we also made a second bathroom. Until then we shared the small bathroom downstairs. The upstairs hall was large enough to put the bath at one end. Tub, shower and double sinks made life easier. The plywood floor and sheet-rocked walls would be fine-tuned later, but we had a second bath.

One interim project was taking off the linoleum in the living room to uncover the original flooring. Below the linoleum Trent found three layers of cardboard covering an inch-thick layer of newspaper. Finally the wood floor emerged. It became apparent that 30' x 14' living room once was two rooms. One end of the living room was covered with pine. Burn marks in a concentrated half circle in the center of the room could not be missed. This probably was the cooking room with the woodstove many years ago. The other part of the living room was maple and in very good condition. We hired a professional to refinish the floor. Stained with a light color and sealed, it looked like new.

In 1983, 15 years after moving in, we finished almost all of the projects. Jason had just left home to enter West Point Military Academy. His room, now shared with Derek, was completely remodeled; wall paper removed, book shelves built-in and plush wall-to-wall carpeting installed. We mailed Jason a piece of the old wall paper as a hint of what was happening. "It'll feel very strange when I come home," he said on the phone.

Kitchen and bath room plywood floors were covered with linoleum. The living room paneling was replaced with sheet rock and wall-to-ceiling book shelves and cabinets were built in to optimize wall space. The downstairs bath, adjoining the kitchen, turned into the pantry/laundry room with a half bath at one end. The stair treads were replaced and all the wood floors refinished. The shell of the old summer kitchen became the back entrance and TV room. House and barn had a new metal roof, so that snow could now slide off easily. A couple fresh coats of white paint covered house and barn; the sheep barn was stained dark brown. The house sparkled when Jason came home for his first leave at Christmas.

Our two-year plan was almost completed. Every space had been remodeled or created. Part of the attached two-story barn was turned into a garage/workshop. The shed was now the sheep barn.

Totally unplanned was a swimming pool. Trent's consulting business was doing very well and I received my share of the sale of the old building in Berlin. We thought that a pool would really enhance the enjoyment of our home. It did.

We installed it above the gardens on the south side of the house. It was surrounded by a fence to keep the sheep and roving dogs out. The sun was heating the pool quickly every spring so that we never used the heater. Pool season lasted from May through October. We had a peaceful little get-away place, just a few steps from our back door.

The master bedroom was left. Except for painting the brown paneled walls white and turning two small adjacent rooms on either side into walk-in closets, it hadn't been touched. We would get to work on it soon.

When we sold the house in 1995, the master bedroom was still waiting, sagging ceiling and all.

◆◆◆

Stay-At-Home Mom

"What do you actually do all day?" Mike, a confirmed bachelor, asked. I had just declined an invitation to play tennis on short notice. I just smiled and moved on. We had met by chance at Mehuron's, the only grocery store in town. It was 1972. Derek (2) was sitting in the grocery cart. Andrea (4) and Jason (6) were walking alongside. I was getting a few food items after picking up Jason at the Bundy School, a Montessori-type school.

A stay-at-home mom was not a popular position to defend. In the early 1970s, the Women's Liberation Movement was in full swing. Women banded together for more workplace and social equality, including pay. The activities of many groups included protests and burning bras. It was in the news daily. The movement is credited with creating the Equal Rights Amendment – ERA – and the forming of the National Organization of Women – NOW, eventually a powerful organization. Most of my contemporaries had career woman as their goal.

But I wouldn't have traded places with anyone. Since Jason was born in 1966, my focus was family. In my mind, being at home with our young children was the best job at that time. I remember my mother always being there for me. No matter what happened during the day I knew I could talk anything over with Mutti, as I called her. Perhaps, because she was a widow raising her two daughters alone, she wanted to make sure she not only provided for us physically but also emotionally. I wanted to do the same for our children.

I didn't have the need to get out of the house. I had fended for myself for five years before getting married. A career could surely wait the few years until all three entered school.

Trent also believed a stable and warm home life would provide a healthy environment for the children. His youth was not so stable or filled with warmth.

As governess, I had spent several years caring for small children. That experience certainly helped living at Pine Hill. I had to rely on myself mostly. Only a couple of our friends had children. Everyone was still in the party mode. My mother was in Germany. She did not have a telephone until the mid 1970s, so I couldn't ask immediate questions or call for help. Trent's mother in nearby Montpelier worked full-time.

How would I really get to know our children's personalities and foibles if I were home only in the evening? I had a weekend job when Jason was one and a very nice high school girl stayed with him. That was about as much time as I was willing to be away from him.

Seeing what Trent's schedule was like, I knew how little I would see our children if I worked full-time. Trent was usually home by 6 p.m. We had dinner together and then the children were off to bed. Time to read bed-time stories.

I knew where the women came from in their thinking. Women had been dismissed as homemakers – no value there and no respect. Most women of that era did not want to tread down that path. My friend Karen had gone from high school straight to college and then married. She hadn't spent any time exploring what she really wanted. Now women's lib made her think and evaluate the future. Shouldn't waste that college education. She couldn't wait to hire babysitters and get out of the house. Her story was probably similar to what was experienced by women across the country.

From an income standpoint, it also didn't make sense to me to take on a job. Earnings were low for women, which eventually changed thanks to women's lib. After paying for childcare, if I could have found a reliable person, I figured my earnings would be about $1 an hour!

Staying home actually saved money. Of course, my friend Mike's eyes would have glazed over had I rattled off some of the following: All meals were cooked from scratch; we saved on gas and wear and tear of our used second car; no dry cleaning bills; I made most of the children's clothes and mine. I also was the barber in residence, being an expert at the Beatles' mob cut.

When I lived in Switzerland, I was a model at a beauty college. The students could practice cutting and perming on my hair. I never had a bad experience. While waiting, I watched students as they gave various haircuts and stored all in my memory. I've been giving all children I worked with haircuts to their parents' delight. No barber shop drama with Heidi. Every two weeks the children and Trent lined up for a trim. I permed and cut my hair also.

Sure, I was the homemaker, but I didn't do it all by myself. The children learned to pitch in from the beginning. Their rooms were their responsibility as soon as they were able. It started with picking up toys and projects. Then they made their beds and were putting away their clean laundry.

We tended the garden together, and it was never considered a chore. Especially once peas and radishes were ready and they could snack while pulling weeds. The children ran out the door with, "You can eat all you want," ringing in their ears.

With everyone helping, we had more time together. We would go floating in the Mad River or on picnics. The all-time favorite was spending time at a friend's swimming pool. "We're done. May we go to Casey's pool now?" one of them would ask. All three learned to doggie paddle from one end of the pool to the other there.

Floating

We often played games like Monopoly or gin rummy. I played records whenever we were home. The children listened to a variety - from rock to musicals to opera. *Mary Poppins* was their favorite, "Play it again, please!" was the usual request. Later it was *Cats*. The only television they watched was Sesame Street and Saturday morning cartoons. "Is it time yet?" became a morning ritual question. I had plenty of reading time on my own during naptime and in the evenings.

The children loved exploring the outdoors. Ours was the only house on the road for years, and it could be seen from all directions. They could go as far as they wanted, as long as they could see the house. When they needed to come home, I rang a large cowbell. Bell ringing to announce dinner became a ritual that I still do today when they are visiting.

Arranging playtimes took up a good chunk of a day. Some friends lived over 20 miles away.

Much time was spent in the kitchen. Jason, Andrea and Derek took turns sitting on the kitchen counter. While I was cooking they were watching and chattering away. Eventually they also wanted to cook. I had my own mini cooking school with three eager students.

Jason started going to school in 1970 when he was four. We hadn't planned that, but it just evolved. Our friends, Sam Whiteside and Lois Melchior, were going to be teachers at a new private school. The Montessori type school was created by Harlow and Martha Carpenter for their two children. Harlow's grandfather started a company that eventually became IBM. The Carpenters owned The Bundy Art Museum in Waitsfield. Harlow was a sculptor and encouraged young artists in the area. When the Carpenters children were school age, the museum turned into the school facility. They asked similar aged children to join the school for a token fee.

Jason was invited, and he was the youngest of the 20, the only pre-kindergartner. We thought it to be good start for Jason as Vermont schools didn't have kindergarten yet. In Vermonters minds, only lazy women sent their children to kindergarten. Carpooling started. With another family from Moretown, we took turns driving the 24 mile round-trip.

Students progressed at their own speed in an open class room arrangement. From the beginning they learned by observing, and by doing projects and research. Instead of answering a student's question, I often heard Lois say,

"See that thick book on the lower shelf. You can read about it in there. Tell me after you found it."

Jason was in kindergarten for two years, seemingly making little progress, except that he loved "going to the Bundy." He played forever with large blocks, adding and taking them down. One day he was passing a table where Sam was working with a student grappling with math. Sam repeated a couple of times, "Ok, how much is it?" Jason slowly walked up to the student and sort of whispered the answer to her.

"I knew it!" Sam told us later. "I could tell he'd been practicing math while pretending not to pay any attention." Jason could no longer pretend, and now was getting assignments like the other students. Occasionally he still played with those blocks.

The years spent at home enabled me to work with Andrea after she was diagnosed as hyperactive. Helping her to function at normal activity levels took much of my attention. I was so thankful that I could be there for her. She joined the Bundy when she was five in 1973. Andrea integrated well and we found that she was a quick learner.

A year later, with only Derek at home, I took on a part-time, home-based sewing job. It turned into a career for me. By 1974, the kindergarten level was part of the school system. When Derek was starting school I spent more time working and eventually opened my own store.

I never regretted being a stay-at-home Mom. I always felt it important to guide children in their early, formative years. Having a like-minded husband definitely helped. Today, I still believe that mothers, or fathers, should be with their young children if they possibly can.

Now I'm proudly watching our children, providing a home like they had for our grandchildren.

◆◆◆

Unexpected Challenge

"Your daughter is autistic. I recommend that you put her in a home for special needs children. Your entire family will be ruined if you keep her." Andrea was just over two years old in the fall of 1970. We had come to the clinic hoping to find help for her. "Talk about it and come back next week."

We headed to our car with Andrea. We didn't talk. Trent was driving. My mind was racing, "What is autism? Give our daughter away?" Half way home in the open countryside, Trent pulled off the road and parked. We looked at each other and simultaneously blurted out, "No! There must be another way."

From the day we brought Andrea home after she was born, my instincts told me that something was not quite right. She did not like to be touched. We couldn't cuddle her the way you like to do with a baby. Even when I was nursing her she strained away.

This continued when she was a toddler. She cried easily and once she started, she couldn't stop. The only solution I came up with was to put her to bed and close the door. Eventually she cried herself to sleep. When she awoke she was quite happy, until the cycle began again; play, get restless and cry. It was hard on all of us. As long as the weather was mild I could take Jason outside to get away from the crying. Andrea also awoke at night, crying for an hour or two until she fell asleep again.

Having worked with infants and toddlers for many years, I knew that this was not normal. I relayed her behavior to our pediatrician at every appointment. His response was always the same, "Don't worry. She seems to be developing just fine. You're probably reading too much into this. See you in a couple of months."

Andrea's development continued to puzzle us. She did not speak coherently and fell often wherever she was walking. Playing outside became a challenge too. Any unexpected movement would bring on a crying spell - even if it was just the wind blowing her light brown hair. I discovered that if she was wearing a hat, no matter the weather, she was content longer. She started wearing a hat, in and out of the house, during all waking hours.

It was hard, if not impossible, for Jason and Andrea to play together. It never lasted more than a few minutes. After Derek was born in July of 1970, being a Mom was more than a full-time job. Jason was four and Andrea two. I tended to the baby, and kept Andrea nearby to interpret her needs. To give Jason equal time, I let him skip naptime. While Andrea and Derek had their mid-day nap, we played games, read books or worked in the gardens together.

By the time Trent came home around six o'clock, I was exhausted. If I had to relay a particularly trying episode with Andrea, I just dissolved into tears. I was an emotional wreck! "How long will life like this continue?" I was asking myself over and over again. Staying at home with the children was what I always wanted. I had a loving husband. Why was I so miserable?

Trent's mother, Nancy, was a counseling psychologist at a mental health clinic in Montpelier. During one of her visits she suggested that we take Andrea to the clinic for an evaluation. She made an appointment for us.

A counselor there prescribed Ritalin. "Come back in two weeks and I'll take another look at her." Ritalin turned her into a zombie. She was clearly drugged and in another world. That was just as hard to witness as her constant crying. We didn't know what to make of it.

At the next visit he declared that she was autistic. When we told him on a subsequent visit that we needed to explore other options, he suggested, "Well, we'll try reducing the dosage. See how that works. Come back in a month. Call me if you need help before then." A lower dosage of Ritalin made her a bit more alert, but sluggish all the time.

The doctor was right in that Andrea's behavior affected our family unit. We started to go on family outings in two cars. Trent and the boys in one and Andrea and I in the other. If Andrea had a crying spell, we never knew what provoked it. I would head home with her so as not to ruin the day for everyone else.

We kept the same routine when grocery shopping. Living in a rural area I shopped once a week for everything. Sometimes she would start crying and, of course, nothing I said or did would make her stop. Once a woman said, "A good spanking is what she needs!" while passing me. After that, we arranged for Trent to be near the grocery store. Should one of her unstoppable crying spells start, Trent would take her home while I finished shopping.

The following spring I was exhausted. I cried easily and felt helpless and hopeless about our daughter. I knew I needed help for myself to get through these trying, endless months. A medical clinic in Burlington, associated with a teaching hospital, was open to the public. I called, relayed how I felt and had an appointment the next day.

After speaking to Dr. Davis, she concluded that I had postpartum depression that could easily be treated. I hadn't heard of this kind of depression before. She explained that my body's hormones did not get back to normal levels after the second baby. Now, after another pregnancy, depression has set in. She called in a colleague and together they ascertained that I was not suicidal and gave me a prescription. "By taking medication for a few weeks, you'll be your normal self soon," she assured me.

Then one of them suggested, "Why don't you bring your daughter here? The clinic has an excellent facility and specialists who work with children."

I drove home with a bottle of pills for myself and an appointment for Andrea. I was so happy, knowing that I was going to get better and we could possibly get help for our little girl. Relief brought me close to tears.

After the children were in bed, Trent and I had a glass of wine while I relayed everything the doctors said. That glass of wine sure made my head spin. The phone rang. It was Dr. Davis, "I neglected to mention that drinking alcohol while taking medication could affect your ability to drive."

"I'm feeling it right now." We both laughed and I thanked her for calling after hours.

The doctor in Burlington wanted to see Andrea while she was taking Ritalin. After that appointment she said, "When you get home, stop the drug and bring her back next week, same time." We had a few trying days after taking her off Ritalin, and she was crying almost non-stop.

Dr. Wright, a child specialist, diagnosed Andrea as hyperactive. This was 1972 and hyperactivity was not commonly known yet. (Later it was called attention deficit hyperactive disorder – ADHD.) "It is unusual in children this early," she continued.

Andrea became the youngest patient to take Taractan, usually given to adults. After only a few days she turned into a happy, non-stop talking two-year-old. Over time, her development started to catch up with things she missed while crying and being in her own world since she was a baby. She interacted with everyone and we could actually hold her for a long period of time. The crying spells appeared less often. Finally, two-and-one-half years after birth we could tell when she was happy by her big smile. Her smile made us happy too. Our daughter finally was a fully functioning little girl, with ups and downs like all children.

There was other goods news. Dr. Wright told us, "She will outgrow hyper- activity with the onset of puberty when her body changes." But we also realized that it meant 10 to 12 years on medication. No one knew much about side effects. Her blood was tested regularly to make sure all was normal. We were concerned about the long-range effect of taking Taractan, although Andrea obviously benefited.

Trent started to search for answers. He learned of Dr. Carl Pfeiffer, MD, in Princeton, New Jersey, known for researching causes and treatment of hyperactivity and the relationship of foods in treatments. Dr. Pfeiffer was convinced that, "For every drug that benefits a patient, there is a natural substance that can achieve the same effect." He was also a biochemist and deeply involved with finding answers. We were hopeful to get help for Andrea. We had to wait seven months for an appointment.

Doctor Pfeiffer examined her irises, tested her fingernails and hair - new methods at the time - among other tests. Results showed shockingly high amounts of zinc and very little copper. Other nutrients were totally out of balance as well. He recommended a high dosage of vitamin C to counterbalance and cleanse her body and other foods to balance her system.

Sugar is a big culprit in processed foods. It uses up valuable vitamin A for digestion and serves no purpose. We began reading labels in earnest. Sugar was everywhere. Items like bread and pasta that were a large part of our diet contained lots of sugar. I had been baking bread for a while but bought commercial loaves when homemade ran out. Now I made sure there always was plenty.

For treats we focused on fruit, easier to digest and does not produce a sugar rush. We did not completely cut out sweets. When my mother sent chocolate bars from

Germany, we spread the consumption over time. A little square of chocolate did not send Andrea into a tailspin.

It was very satisfying when we could see how our lifestyle reverberated with the children. During the weekly trip to the grocery store I let them know to "Pick anything you want for a snack." They promptly headed to the fruit department to choose their treat.

I was cooking all meals mostly from scratch and that helped to eliminate preservatives, colorings, flavorings and multitudes of additives. At the time no one knew that those additives were having negative effects on the body's system. The entire family benefited from this emphasis on clean foods.

Step by step we were able to reduce Andrea's medication. It wasn't simple. We experimented with reducing her dosage during school breaks. Andrea's medication was lowered by a tenth. Within a couple of days we could tell if her body was ready or not. After three years she did well on a small maintenance dose.

We were so pleased to have found a solution for Andrea that we freely talked about it. It was a huge mistake. When she started going to the Bundy School, we relayed our experience to the teachers. We included her noon pill in her lunch box. The result was that Andrea was teased mercilessly by the other pupils. From a distance I witnessed it often. When someone started to cry, a fellow student cooed, "Oh, what's the matter?" and patted the girl on the shoulder, etc. When Andrea started to cry, a friend said, "Oh, go take your pill, hi,hi!" It hurt me to see this, but I know it hurt Andrea even more. All I could do was to give a long hug later to let her know I loved her.

Trent and I decided to take Andrea out of the small environment of that private school where everybody knew she was taking medication. We enrolled her in the elementary school in Moretown for a fresh start. We changed her medication schedule so that she didn't need to take a pill during her school day. We hoped she would be fine.

It could have worked. Unfortunately, only a few weeks later two of the leaders in the teasing department also transferred to Moretown. So Andrea had to deal with that calculated teasing for years. It did not help her to make friends.

She experienced happier times at home. Once she was on the right medication, she integrated quickly into everyday life. During the following years we slowly got our family unit back. Derek and Andrea became buddies. It took Jason longer to come out of the shell he'd retreated to when Andrea was crying. He was almost three years old when she was born. Andrea didn't turn into the sibling he was ready to love.

From a zombie, Andrea turned into a focused, curious child. She showed a voracious appetite for reading and learning. Just like the boys, we encouraged and support all she wanted to do. Music was one of her main interests. After starting piano lessons, she quickly changed to the flute instead. She was in the school band and continued playing well after her school years. I loved listening when she practiced.

She had the gift of perfect pitch and was a beautiful soprano. She loved singing. I don't know which she was drawn to more - flute or voice. When she was self-conscious about doing suggested exercises by her voice teacher, she went to the sheep barn. There, she let go and sang to the sheep and cats! I opened the kitchen window so that I could listen too.

Andrea also became a well-coordinated athlete. She gave up ice hockey when she was ten, she said, "I don't want to be the only girl." So she turned to track and field, cross-country running and skiing. She was on the high school varsity squads in all three sports. Andrea was very intelligent and received the Top Student Athlete award when she graduated in 1986.

Farm and Garden

———————•——•———————

Rosemary, sage and thyme started it all.

Our friend Jackie Rose stopped by our rental house. She handed me a small carton filled with rosemary, sage and thyme plants she had dug up from her garden. Standing on the front stoop, Jackie was pointing down, "This is perfect for a little herb garden. You have a sunny location here and they'll do well. Just keep them from drying out." We had been married a few weeks and just moved into the house in the center of Waitsfield. I was excited. It hadn't occurred to me to plant some herbs although I was using fresh ones in my cooking almost daily.

I was a city girl. Up to this point my gardening experience consisted of watering my mother's geraniums in an outdoor flower box on our living room's window sill. But I knew enough to know that the compact dirt by our entrance was not garden soil. Although Trent had helped his grandfather in the garden when he was small, he hadn't paid attention to gardens since. He did remember the peas he snatched at a neighboring farm and how sweet they tasted. Neither of us had gardening on our to-do list.

I didn't have a driver's license yet, so Trent drove me to the farm supply store. Along with some topsoil and dry manure, I also bought a small shovel and a couple of parsley and chive plants to complete my little herb garden. We both were getting excited about gardening and made plans for growing some vegetables the following year. "Let's plant lettuce and peas," Trent said.

"And tomatoes and green beans," was my contribution.

As soon as we were back at the house I went to work. I mixed the soil and planted the herbs according to size - rosemary, the one that would grow the tallest, in the back and thyme in the front. I was looking forward to fresh chives from my own garden.

In early October we moved to a larger rental we had found next to the post office in nearby Warren. I dug up the herb plants and replanted them right away at our new place. I hoped that they had enough time to get acclimated before it snowed.

All but the rosemary came back to life in the spring. The Vermont winter was just too cold for that plant to survive.

Trent rented a rototiller to break up the compact grass for a garden space. He had noticed that the grass was doing particularly well on the slope down to the Mad River that was flowing behind the house. That's where he established the vegetable bed. Everything thrived, and we had plenty for the two of us. Jason was born in January and was not eating regular food yet.

Jessie Cota, our landlord, stopped by one day, just to chat. He came in the house and from the kitchen window he noticed our vegetable garden. "Don't the plants look well?" I said.

"Ha," he chuckled, "They should. You planted them right smack on top of the septic tank." We moved the vegetable bed a few feet away from there the following year.

Then came the year we bought our house in Moretown. We didn't move until the end of August. The herbs moved with us again. I transplanted them in front of the small shed that eventually became the sheep barn, just a few steps from the house. I figured the southern exposure would help the plants to make it through the below zero winter months. It was too late to start a garden of any kind. But we had the winter ahead for making plans.

Besides having a new baby to care for, Trent and I worked constantly on the indoor remodeling projects. In the evenings our conversation often ventured towards spring and gardening. We had some outside clean-up projects waiting for us. Across the driveway from the house was a partially fallen down barn. "As soon as the snow is gone, I'll tear it down and burn it," Trent said. "It'll be a good spot for our vegetable garden." Then he said, "Let's get some chickens too. The shed will be their coop to be safe at night."

I was surprised, "You want to be a farmer?" I asked.

"Oh, sure. I watched my granddad. There's not much to it. And why not? We have the land, so let's grow as much food as we possibly can. I'll be in charge of the chickens and you grow the vegetables."

Trent continued, "Remember the Nearings?"

Trent was recalling the book "Living the Good Life" by Helen and Scott Nearing. The Nearings were early proponents of living off the land. They bought large parcels of forested land in Vermont in the 1940s and became self sufficient. They wrote about their experience in the book in 1954. Scott and Helen Nearing truly lived off the land. They basically did everything, including building their home and other buildings with rocks they collected on the land.

By the time we bought our home years later, the Nearings had moved to Maine. Vermont was no longer rural enough.

"Well," I said, "luckily we don't have to build a house. Chickens and vegetables will be plenty to do, along with everything else."

I agreed that we could do as much as possible to have plenty of food on the table for our family. Food was our security blanket. Trent and I needed to know that the kitchen cupboards and the refrigerator were well stocked.

I never had enough to eat in my early childhood, because there simply wasn't any to be had in post-World-War-II Berlin. Trent also recalled always being hungry. His father expected Trent's mother to feed him and his three siblings on a very meager food budget. "We ate lots of lettuce and mayo sandwiches. They were very small. Dinner wasn't much better. I was always hungry."

Spring came and the melting snow kept the ground wet into April. "That's actually a good thing," Trent said. "I won't have to worry about anything catching fire when I'm burning the pile of wood from the barn." A few of the old board were salvageable, and the rest created a high mound to be burned. The fire created immense heat, but it was far enough away from the house so that I didn't worry. The barn had been on one of the few level areas and would be a good site for a garden indeed.

So far, gardening had not been a big challenge. I just followed directions on seed packets, but I felt that I needed to learn more about soils, area particulars and what grows best where. I was looking for information every time I drove into town. Finally I came across a thick gardening book, "The Rockwell's Guide to Successful Gardening." The over 1,000-page-tome covered everything from vegetables to trees and flowers in detail. It became my constant 'go-to' source.

My original plan for a vegetable garden was modest. I figured that a 12x12-foot plot of dirt would supply us well. Besides the standard peas, lettuce and carrots, I also wanted to plant vegetables that I missed, like kohlrabi, leek and brussels sprouts. I couldn't find seeds or plants anywhere and was elated when I found them in a Burpee catalog.

Our vegetables were growing exceedingly well. We were impressed with the fertile land. Our closest year-round neighbors, the Howes, lived a mile down the hill from us. Three generations were working on their dairy farm. One time grandfather Howe told Trent, "The barn that you cleared off where your garden is now - that was the Farnsworths' cow barn." That explained the fertile land.

As I was not obsessed with housework, I was also not meticulous with weeding. Making the beds every morning seemed like a waste of time. They would just get messed up the following night. Rather than covering the beds up with comforters, I pulled the sheets back and let the bed air all day, straightening all neatly, ready for another good night sleep.

Weeding the garden was similar. As soon as weeds were pulled, it seemed as if new ones emerged instantly. When seedlings sprouted, I weeded carefully and then covered the ground with black plastic. That was a good practice in northern Vermont; it kept heat and moisture in the ground and weeding to a minimum. I didn't have to spend my time with this redundant chore and had more time to spend in the flower garden.

I had no idea how much I would love gardening. Just like cooking, it became a daily must-do for me. We moved several times and establishing flower and vegetable gardens was as important as arranging the furniture.

I loved working in the garden with my bare hands. I tried wearing gloves to save my fingernails, but it just didn't work. The gloves came off every time I needed to really grab a weed. When I put the gloves on again, the dirt got inside and ground into my fingers. What a nuisance. Eventually I didn't bother putting them on at all.

Baby chicks soon arrived. Jason was delighted and watched Trent build a fenced area outside the small shack that was attached to the large two-story barn. Once the chickens were grown, they roamed around the garden and yard; in the evening they found their way into the coop. Trent made sure the coop was secure at night from foxes and skunks, the most common predators around.

The children were in charge of checking for and gatherings eggs in the morning. There always was a chicken or two in the freezer, which I found very reassuring.

As Trent had promised, raising chickens was not complicated. My patience was tested only once. One spring, the arrival of baby chicks proved to be too early. As the mailman handed the box to me he said, "I hope you have plenty of heating lamps."

April night temperatures were still in the single digits. Too cold in the barn for just hatched chicks, even with heat lamps. What to do? Trent rigged an 8x10 plywood board with two heat lamps in our basement. Although cool, it was always well above freezing there. The thirty chicks had a comfy home, but it wouldn't be for long.

Baby chicks in the living room

A couple of weeks later we had a horrendous spring snowstorm, cutting off the power across northern Vermont. The power company predicted an outage of four to six days. Without heat lamps, the chicks were too young to survive in the cool basement.

The baby chicks moved upstairs into the living room. We were in the process of remodeling the room at the time. All furniture had been moved out. The living room had a wood stove, now our only heat source. It was quite a sight, seeing the chicks cavorting on their platform in our living room. Trent added a high edge to the platform so that they couldn't fall off.

We could hear their "peeps" in every room. Power was restored after a week. Just in time. The chicks started testing their wings and would soon be flying about the room. I was happy to see them move into the shed.

The children grew and with it the need for more vegetables. I planted more and also more vegetable varieties. The garden expanded a couple of feet in all directions every year, mostly uphill. Eventually I had two gardens, one behind the other. Because of the sloping land we made a low wall into the hillside and leveled the land beyond for the second garden. From spring through autumn we harvested an abundance of fresh veggies; I rarely bought any produce.

Flower beds were expanding every summer just like the vegetable garden. I love flowers and simply could not plant enough. Perennials and annuals, in the ground and in pots, were everywhere: along the house foundation, in front of the vegetable beds, all around the swimming pool and mingling in the herb garden. Daisies, roses, delphiniums, and others were thriving in the Vermont climate. Any spare time I had was spent in the flower garden. It was my meditation.

Growing rosemary was more of a challenge. I tried wrapping the plant with burlap, but it didn't make it through the winter. The following fall I transplanted one to a large pot and brought it into the house. The plant shriveled up and died after a month. I tried this several times with the same outcome. Finally, instead of planting rosemary in the garden, I opted to start it in a pot. I positioned it in the center of the herb garden and brought the pot into the house before a hard frost. That did it. My rosemary stayed vigorous and grew larger every summer.

Jason, Andrea and later Derek helped with planting, weeding and watering as soon as they were old enough. They were getting lettuce or tomatoes when it was time to make a salad for dinner. There usually was a radish to pull or pea to snap off for snacking along the way.

I was not a fan of canning and tried to grow just enough for our needs. When I did have extras, I preferred freezing. We had two freezers in the barn. When there was an abundance of tomatoes, I quickly cooked a sauce and was happy to retrieve a frozen packet in the winter.

Applesauce and cider also filled the freezers. The house originally came with one acre. A couple of years later we were able to buy an additional five acres that included an apple orchard. Those apple trees were well over a hundred years old. We had everything from early to very late ripening varieties; and always more than we could possibly eat. In the fall, we had our own cider festival. Friends and their families joined us for making cider. The children were busy picking apples for the better part of a day. The adults were manning the apple press and produced gallon after gallon of cider. They could take home as much as they wanted and we still had plenty to last us through the winter.

Generally, Trent stuck to farming and I stayed with gardening. There were a couple of distinct exceptions. Trent wanted to grow grapes to make his own wine. He planted a vineyard with Marechal Foch grape stock, recommended for our cold conditions by the agriculture department at Cornell University. The vineyard flourished with minimal winter losses. After a couple of years, everyone helped to harvest the red clusters.

Trent had set up all wine-making equipment in the basement. Only the jugs of grape juice were carried to the living room for the fermenting phase because the basement was just not warm enough. Eventually Trent made a very respectable dry red wine. He also experimented with making apple wine. He produced an excellent dry white wine that resembled a Riesling, his favorite German wine.

Rabbits were the next livestock addition. They were easy to raise in elevated cages and very prolific. Trent took care of them, including butchering. When I planned a rabbit dinner, he delivered one prepped and ready for cooking at the kitchen door. Jason and Derek always helped and watched. In later years that turned into an unexpected bonus.

During Jason's first year at West Point, all Plebes (freshmen) had survival training. Once they were sent into the woods for 24 hours with only a knife, a canteen of water, a book of matches and a live rabbit. Groans all around. Plebes fanned out into the forest in groups of eight. "Man, I'm gonna be starving when we get back," echoed through the woods.

Many overnights in our surrounding woods made Jason comfortable in the wild. He sprang into action and supervised his comrades to cut down pine branches to build an overnight shelter. Then he split his group into foragers and gatherers. He showed them edible plants like ferns and dandelion. They returned to their makeshift camp loaded with plenty of supplies: firewood, berries, roots and greens.

"What about the rabbit?" they asked. Jason did what he had watched Trent do years ago - killed the rabbit, cleaned and skinned it and had it ready to be roasted over a fire his crew was building. The city boys were grossed out, "We're supposed to eat that?" As the rabbit slowly roasted over the fire and the smell of grilling meat filled the air, they were getting excited over dinner prospects. Along with a salad of greens and chopped roots, dinner was satisfying indeed. None of the other groups, who could smell dinner roasting, ate anything; they just drank water until they could get back to civilization.

Derek, by the way, also became a leader after he'd been following his brother for years. He spent a month at an Outward Bound camp in Colorado. Part of the experience is spending time alone in the woods. Campers were dropped off by the side of the road in the wilderness and picked up there again after 48 hours. Derek was completely comfortable in his skin and helped his fellow city-slicker campers not to freak out as they found spots for their solitary experience. After that they looked to him at all times. It was an invaluable growing–up time for him.

Like any respectable farm, we also had an abundance of cats around. They were Andrea's favorite. She spent hours with them, especially when there was a new litter of kittens. They lived in the barn and were totally self-sufficient. We just made sure they had access to fresh water in the winter. Cat food was also available to them, but they partook very little. I guess they found plenty of mice to feast on.

The cats rarely came into the house. In the summer they sometimes ventured in through an open door. Then they made a quick round through all rooms and dashed back out. Andrea's favorite, Bright Eyes, was the exception. She was quite comfortable lounging in Andrea's room, keeping her company. But, come evening, she was ready to head towards the barn again.

In 1974, after we bought the additional acreage, Trent started our sheep herd. "The sheep will have plenty of fresh grass; we'll only need some hay for the snowy winter months." We both liked lamb roasts and would now have some from our own supply.

Trent built and repaired fences every summer with Jason's help. All but a small lawn section on the south side of the house was fenced and we could move the sheep around to different areas.

Derek's task in the summer was to mow the lawn. First we had the standard push mover that was hard to maneuver over the uneven ground. Later he drove the old Craftsman lawn tractor at break-neck speed around trees, rocks and gardens once a week.

Andrea, even when very little, became the resident leaf-raker. One chilly fall evening, as the sky began to grow darker, Trent couldn't find her. But there she was, under the Macintosh apple tree, still raking. Everyone loved great leaf bonfires alongside the road.

Moving a high pile of firewood that was dumped at the end of our driveway was the least favorite task of all. The wood usually arrived on a weekend when Trent was working. It was up to the four of us to carry and stack the logs behind the barn. We rotated carrying and stacking. We got it done as quickly as possible so that we didn't have to look at that pile of wood.

Least favorite chore

In the fall, we culled the now grown lambs, keeping promising ewe lambs for breeding. The herd was growing and eventually we decided to keep just nine ewes and a ram, a manageable size.

We sent the sheep to the Howe's farm down the hill for slaughtering and processing. The meat packages were traded for other meats like pork and beef. Some were traded for firewood and services like snowplowing. The rest went into our freezer.

Tending sheep was definitely a family affair. Jason checked their fresh water supply. Derek and Andrea fed them hay during the winter months. Everyone was watching for signs of lambing in the spring. I became the veterinarian in residence when a ewe couldn't deliver lambs without help. If a lamb needed to be bottle fed, Jason, Andrea and Derek took turns without grumbling.

Young lambs also were entertainment for many months. If I didn't see the children around, I'd find them behind the barn, watching lambs on the hillside. Lambs were chasing each other endlessly up and down the sloping ground, collapsing for a couple of minutes and then starting all over again.

◆◆◆

Shepherd

———————•———•———

"Let's take this one. She is so cute." That's how our sheep herding started. Since we moved to Moretown, Trent had added chickens and rabbits to the farm part of our property.

In the spring of 1974, we drove to Henry Swayze's sheep farm with our three children to buy a ewe. Trent was planning: "We'll start with one, then add more. I'll build a fence. The grass on the hillside will be kept down." He added "It'll be simple."

I grew up in the center of Berlin. All I knew of sheep was that two are happier than one alone, lamb roasts are delicious and lamb's wool makes scratchy knee socks.

The cute lamb was an orphan and needed to be bottle fed for a couple of months. "I'll help," our three children, Derek (4), Andrea (6) and Jason (8) promised in unison with sparkling, pleading eyes. We named our lamb Serena. Henry Swayze gave us a couple of milk-filled beer bottles with nipples attached. "That should get you started," he said. "Remember, the worst thing you can do is over-feed the lamb. Make it half milk/half water for at least another week."

We decided the turns everyone would take bottle feeding Serena. Trent was first. He climbed into the pen in the barn, scooped Serena up and offered the nipple end of the bottle. She was not sure of us or the bottle at first. Sprinkling a bit of milk on her nose was all it took. She went for the nipple and didn't let go until the bottle was empty. Our children took their turns in two-hour intervals without having to be reminded. They didn't want to miss their time alone with Serena.

Bottle time

We learned as we went along. Serena would get diarrhea if we increased the milk ratio too quickly. She actually left my mother-in-law, Nancy, speechless. On one of Nancy's visits, Serena had diarrhea and was inside the house, running around with a diaper on. When Nancy walked into the living room she almost dropped her tea cup, "Trent!" she screamed, "What are you into now?"

Soon our orphan was off the bottle and eagerly nibbling on emerging grass in the pasture. We realized that one little lamb barely made a dent in keeping the grass down. We went back to Swayze's farm for another. We spread more grass seeds around the pastures to improve the quality. New grass would be sprouting the following April.

During that first year we discovered that our area, Moretown Common, was once entirely populated by people from Scotland. Most of the farms, including ours, were sheep farms in the 1800s. Actually, Vermont had more sheep than any other state during that era.

Lambing should be simple. Sheep have taken care of themselves for centuries. However, they are not the hardy self-sufficient animals they once were. Breeding for either wool or meat quality has made the ewes more vulnerable. We were raising *Cheviots* because they usually had twins and *Romney Marsh*, known for their long staple wool.

We added six young ewes and a ram to our flock. Our herd kept grass and weeds down. The ram did his job of mating with all the ewes. Next spring we could expect our own lambs.

For some reason, to this day I have not figured out why our lambs were born during the coldest spells. During lambing I spent many cold hours in the barn when it was 30 below zero outside.

Our first lambing season came off without any complications. Each ewe had twins. We didn't have any orphans to bottle feed. Within a couple of weeks our herd expanded to 19. It was very crowded in our small barn.

In late spring the sheep were shorn of their winter coat. Spinners in the area were ready to buy the wool the minute the fleeces were off. All lambs were going to be slaughtered in the fall.

The following spring lambing turned out differently. Each ewe had triplets. The first two ewes were doing fine on their own. The next one had two lambs and I could tell another one was coming, but there was no progress.

I called Steve Pattison, the only veterinarian in a 50-mile radius. "The lamb may need to be turned. You'll have to help. Better you than Trent. You have smaller hands. Sneak both hands into the uterus. Locate the head. If indeed it is facing the wrong way, you'll have to turn it."

"What if I hurt the lamb or the ewe?" I worried. I pushed back my sweater sleeves and carefully slid my hand into the rear of the ewe. She gave no reaction. My other hand followed. Sure enough, I needed to turn the lamb. In my mind I kept hearing Steve's voice, "Make sure both forefeet are framing the head. Gently move the lamb around until the head is pointing towards you." With the next contraction, I carefully pulled the lamb. After about 20 minutes, which seemed like eternity, another triplet was complete. "Yeah!" I was very proud of having saved the lamb. I couldn't wait to show off my accomplishment to the family.

Then, one morning, lambing did not go so well. A ewe lay down, strained and strained – nothing happened. I waited an hour. No lambs. I called our vet. "You have to go in and try to pull out the lambs," he said.

I explored and could feel three lambs. But nothing ever happened during contractions. I ran back into the kitchen and called the vet again. "Nothing is moving!" I was desperate to do the right thing.

"Keep trying," he advised.

Back to the barn. The ewe was still down. I felt the lambs again. I had to admit to myself that they were dead. An odd calm came over me. I was shaking but not from the cold. It came from deep within me.

Another call to Steve. "You'll have to pull the carcasses out," he told me. I was shocked. Me? Pull carcasses out of one of our ewes?

He continued, "They may come out in pieces. Hard to tell how long they've been dead. It may be too late to save the ewe. You'll have to try or you won't forgive yourself. I can be there this afternoon."

I ran back to the barn hoping to see a change. I felt so bad for the ewe. She looked at me silently with very large eyes. I couldn't give in to this feeling of helplessness. I tried not to think about what I was doing as I pulled legs and bodies out. Uncontrollable sobs overcame me as I looked at the remains.

When Steve came he took one look at the ewe and said, "She's dying."

Did we miss any signs? Would we have noticed a stoic ewe sooner with fewer sheep to manage? Trent and I decided to downsize our herd, hoping to raise a healthy flock every year. We kept Serena and six other ewes.

During the following nineteen springs, many healthy lambs were born. During lambing I always went to the barn with a bit of apprehension, hoping that the animals would be all right. They were. I was very happy when I didn't have to step into the shoes of a vet again.

◆◆◆

Baker

———————•—•———————

When I close my eyes I can still smell freshly baked loaves of bread lined up on a cooling rack.

It was December 1964, and I had just arrived in Vermont after a bumpy train ride from New York for a winter of working and skiing at the Sugarbush Ski Resort. My friend Judy, whom I would be working for at the slope-side day care center, met me at the train station in Waterbury.

Once underway she said, "On the way we'll stop by my friends, the Von Trapps in Waitsfield, to say hello."

"Von Trapp, as in the Trapp Family Singers?" I asked.

"Yes, Werner and most of his brothers and sisters are in the Waitsfield area. The Baroness, Maria, has a lodge in Stowe." I knew their family history, how they fled Nazi occupied Austria, from a book I had read in Germany. I began thinking of the anti-German sentiments that have come my way when I was living in Switzerland. "Maybe the Von Trapps will be more like others I also had met, with a great capacity for living in the present, and treating me like any other person," I was hoping.

It was already dark when we arrived at their farmhouse and I got out of the car. A familiar, but long missed, aroma came my way. When Judy opened the front door, the smell of freshly baked bread came at me full force. Oh, what memories!

Growing up in Berlin, the aroma of baking bread was in the air every morning. We had a bakery on every block and knew when the bread was out of the oven to get the freshest loaf. In the early post-World-War-II years, bread was often the only food we had for days. They were hefty whole wheat or rye loaves; they had substance and were satisfying (if we were lucky to get enough). But bakeries were the producers of this life staple, not housewives.

Although, at twenty-two, I was an experienced chef, bread baking was not on my resume. That December evening changed all that.

The front door opened into the warm kitchen where the family just finished supper. After friendly introductions, Barbara, the older daughter, and her sister went back to helping with the dishes. The four boys headed back to the barn, "to finish our daily chores," Werner said as he followed them out the door.

I needn't have worried about the Von Trapps attitude. Werner, in his late forties, the public singing days long behind him, was now a farmer and family man. He was a gentle man with a twinkle in his eyes. People mattered, not the past. (Many years later Barbara was working for me at my *Heidi of Vermont* store.)

I was admiring the loaves on the kitchen counter and asked, "You made these?"

"Sure," Werner's Austrian wife Erika nodded. "I've been baking bread ever since I moved here." Erika expounded about yeasts, rising, resting and moisture in the oven. All of it went right over my head. But I knew for sure, "Someday, I'll make my own bread!"

As a homemaker a few years later, tired of the Wonder Bread-type offerings, my baking journey began. I started with a recipe in *Fannie Farmer's* cookbook. The aroma filling the house was welcomed. The bread was tasty, but not the hefty loaf I was aiming for.

I began hounding book stores and finally found a thin paperback, *Uncle John's Original Bread Book* by John Rahn Braue (Pyramid Books, 1969.) This book answered all my novice baker's questions and became my bread bible. The recipes included yeast and sourdough breads from French bread to Russian pumpernickel.

Finally I had help with making baguettes, batards and crusty rolls. Sometimes the bread turned into different shapes. My children had their favorites, "Oh please, make another Easter bunny." That request was easy to fulfill with a rye dough I developed.

I bought different flours and yeasts, and cultivated my starter in the refrigerator. When I could not find what I needed, I ordered flours or grains by mail and headed to the kitchen as soon as they arrived.

As my children grew up, freshly baked bread often greeted them coming home from school. Bread baking was arranged around my work, school events and sport schedules. It became easier as I grew braver. Rising dough is forgiving. If I couldn't be in the kitchen when it was time to bake, I punched the dough down, covered it up to let it rise again and baked it later. Occasionally I had to learn that that there is a point of 'no more rising' and I would have to start over.

Friends took note at our dinner table. "Where did you find this bread?" Patti asked.

"I made it."

"Oh, sure," she said.

"No, really. I have an easy recipe."

"I'd like to give it a try. The bread is fabulous! Would you show me how?" she asked.

I invited Patti and two other friends for a bread-making session the following week. Non-sourdough French bread is the quickest to make from start to finish, so I planned to make four loaves.

I pulled our expandable dining table into the center of my spacious kitchen. The table gave us room to gather around and for a hands-on experience. My friends mixed flour and yeast and took turns kneading, spreading lots of flour onto the floor in the process. After the dough had risen, we each shaped a loaf, put them on baking sheets and set them aside for another rise. After the loaves had risen again sufficiently, we cut diagonal slits into the tops with a razor blade and slid the baking sheets with the loaves into the preheated oven.

While the dough was rising, and later baking, we cleaned up and then sat around the table and talked 'bread': where to order yeast, different flours, or a baking stone for the oven, and more.

I had made a tomato soup the previous day and a mixed salad before the group arrived. We shared one of the cooled off loaves at lunch and they agreed, "This is the tastiest bread ever!" I sent them home with a loaf each and several other bread recipes to expand their baking prowess. I held a monthly baking session in my kitchen for quite a while.

Our children are bakers in their own right now and I have learned from them. "Mom, just throw ice cubes onto the bottom of the oven They'll do it all." No more spritzing the oven, or pans of water to create moisture.

A trip to Italy enriched my bread making. We were in the province of Liguria on the Italian coast, the birthplace of focaccia. There is a Focacceria on every block, sometimes two; fresh focaccia was constantly put on the shelves. And the choices were endless... with onions, with fresh pesto, with grapes, with garlic...and many more options. Oh, the aroma in the air...heavenly! The focaccias tasted nothing like the store-bought U.S. versions. I collected recipes and tips that the bakers readily shared; "...anda don'ta baka de breada too a longa."

When I pull a rosemary and garlic focaccia out of the oven now, it smells and tastes just like I remember.

◆◆◆

The Bag Lady

---◆━◆━◆---

All I was looking for was a little pin money.

In 1974, a friend offered me a part-time job. Bonnie had a leather and canvas bag business. She sold her creations at weekend craft fairs. Local women sewed these bags at home, getting paid per piece.

Jason and Andrea were in school and Derek, the youngest, would be starting the following year. I had been sewing my own clothes since I was a teenager. I knew I would be able to sew bags for Bonnie. I agreed to her offer.

Bonnie introduced me to the routine the following week at her house. She cut pieces for the different designs. I took home the materials and needed thread and webbing for the bag handles. When the bags were completed, I had to bring them back for inspection. I got paid if no do-overs were needed. She also said, "If you like, you can also help with the prep work for the leather bags here at my studio."

I took materials for five bags home. My Singer sewing machine was set up in the spare downstairs bedroom. After Jason and Andrea went off to school the following morning, I settled at the machine.

Most bags were the size of the common LL Bean bags, and all seams were straight. Sewing was easy and fast. I had to slow down only when I came to corners, where the material became several layers thick. Sometimes I had to stop and move the material very slowly or the needle would skip a stitch. If I forgot to go slowly, the needle broke.

Derek was curious and watched the entire process standing by my chair. Five bags were done in a couple of hours. He came with me when I drove to Bonnie's to see if the bags passed inspection.

My workmanship was flawless. From then on the routine was to get the prepped materials and return the finished bags weekly. I bought a commercial sewing machine in a second-hand shop. The machine handled the thick corner parts of the bags with ease, so the time needed to finish a bag was almost cut in half.

Bonnie called when she needed help with the leather products. I spent many hours gluing parts of leather for bags and belts together that later would be sewn over. It was routine work that didn't capture my imagination.

I liked working with canvas. It was colorful, easy to handle and turn into attractive and sturdy bags. I thought the bags should reach a wider market than the crowds at fairs in Vermont.

"Bonnie, there isn't anything like this in stores. You could widen your market," I suggested.

"Nah, that's too time-consuming. I don't want to go around finding new outlets," was her reaction.

"I'll go if you like. I think that could add another dimension to your business."

"I'm not interested in that."

I brought up the subject several times during the ensuing year. My enthusiasm hadn't changed. My formal education in Germany culminated with a retail and wholesale merchandising degree at a business school in Berlin. I kept thinking about the possibilities for the bags.

Trent and I often talked about going into business myself. "You're good at this. You can do this," he kept saying.

"There really isn't any room in the house to set it all up."

"Well, you can use the upstairs hall. I'll make a cutting table out of plywood. You can store materials underneath."

"But if I have to find outlets, I don't have enough time for sewing!"

"You produce and I'll go all over Vermont and beyond to stores. I'll take one day a week off from real estate and be your salesman."

That could work I thought. I didn't want to go to fairs, because that was Bonnie's territory and I wanted to respect that. Besides, I didn't want to be at fairs on weekends when the children would be off from school.

Finally I gave in to Trent's nudging. In the spring, I gave Bonnie my notice and told her my plan. "You're my best producer! How can you do this to me?" I wasn't going to be persuaded.

"I would have continued working for you if you'd let me go to and expand the retail market for you. Also, a raise would have made a difference."

I had asked for a raise a couple of times. I only made minimum wage if there were no delays while sewing. Every time Bonnie had answered "I can't pay more."

Now I planned in earnest. I started designing a couple tote bags on paper. I made lists of what I needed:

canvas, lining, threads, zippers, canvas webbing and boxes for shipping. Then I realized that I needed more money than we had to get started. "Get a loan," Trent told me.

My business head kicked in. I remembered my lack of enthusiasm for business school in Berlin. The school's curriculum covered all aspects of the wholesale and retail business - from origin of raw products to business planning and accounting. Now I could apply all that I had learned. I planned everything to the penny: costs to produce a bag; what they would sell for; what could be sold the first year; the projected profits.

I needed a name for this new business. Many dinner discussions centered on possible names. Everyone voted and by unanimous decision it became *Heidi of Vermont.*

With a six-page business proposal in hand, I met with the loan officer of the Howard Bank in Waitsfield. He reviewed it while I was sitting across his desk. The office was very quiet, and I felt nervous. "What if the bank doesn't make this kind of a loan?" Finally he looked up, "How much do you need?"

"Five hundred dollars. I can pay it back in six months."

"We're having a board meeting tomorrow. I'll let you know."

Two days later, a Friday, he called, "It's approved. You can get a check this afternoon." I was officially in business. I couldn't wait to tell Trent.

When Trent arrived home that evening he announced, "I've agreed to be salesman at a new housing development in Essex Junction (outside of Burlington)." That was good news indeed! Our income potential was looking up in this down economy.

"That is terrific." I was really happy for Trent. Then I asked, "What about the part of being my salesman?"

"You'll just have to manage. I cannot take any time off now."

Back to the drawing board. I reworked my schedule. I would sew five days a week and every other week I could take one of those days to call on businesses.

Every morning after the children were off to school I went to work. The cutting table in the upstairs hall also turned into my designing and planning desk. I ordered canvas in 20 yard rolls, which UPS delivered to our rural setting. Navy blue, crimson red, kelly green and natural-colored canvas was stored under the table.

My bags were lined with bright blue waterproof rip-stop nylon, a very light material used for parachutes, sails and hot air balloons. Lining the bags made for a very clean interior appearance. The totes were a little dressier than the standard LL Bean bag. All bags were in two-color combinations: red with blue trim, natural with navy and kelly green with navy trim. Some totes were a single color with white canvas webbing handles. At first I made a small and a large tote bag. I also made a log carrier that turned out to be a very reliable seller.

I stayed busy until 1p.m. It was time to get Derek, who was now in kindergarten.

I called my favorite stores for appointments to show the bags. On my travel days, Derek could play hooky and come with me because I couldn't be sure that I would be back by 1:00. "You'll have to be very still when I make my sales pitch. Do you think you can do this?" He nodded.

On the morning of my first scheduled road trip, northern Vermont had a late spring snowstorm. The countryside was covered with a 12-inch blanket of white fluff. I was tempted to cancel the appointment. I had a pro and con discussion with myself. "If I'm going to make this business work, I better not let a snowstorm dictate my schedule," I reasoned.

Derek and I went on our way. I was keeping my fingers crossed that I made the right decision as I slowly drove the four miles from our house to the main road.

My first appointment was at The Mayfair in Burlington, an upscale women's clothing store. The owners were very receptive and ordered a dozen tote bags. They also asked me to design a tennis bag in natural with an orange pocket for the racket. I agreed to bring it along when I delivered their order. The Mayfair ordered a dozen when they saw the prototype. The store became a steady client.

Derek behaved perfectly throughout the appointment and I was very happy with my first order. Our reward for this successful outing was a stop at Howard Johnsons. Even though it was snowing, we both feasted on luscious strawberry ice cream parfaits. We were home in time to pick up Jason and Andrea from school by 3p.m.

At the dinner table the success of my first order was celebrated. Andrea suggested, "How about green and purple?" as a new color combination.

"I don't have purple."

"How about yellow and black?" came from Jason who chose black for everything.

"I don't have yellow either, but that's a good suggestion. I'll order yellow." That's how it went.

My schedule worked. I realized that I liked having my own business. My head was spinning with ideas for new bag designs.

I was able to add more accounts. I bought additional canvas colors and *Heidi of Vermont* cloth labels to be sewn into every bag. In the early fall, I placed my first mail-order ad, featuring the log carrier, in the *New England Journal* magazine. It proved to be a good investment; orders came in by mail and phone.

I designed a catalog of tote and duffel bags to be included with the mail orders.

Retail clients suggested other businesses to call on. A relative carried my tote and duffel bags at his marina in Maryland. One of our friends was manager of a women's clothing and sports shop in Florida and placed an order. The business grew. My upstairs hall was getting crowded with stored materials, leaving little space for cutting.

In the fall of 1976, I took the plunge and rented an upstairs space in the Mad River Green Shopping Center in the business district of Waitsfield. The buildings looked like the traditional two-storied red barns dotting the Vermont countryside. The shopping center included a hardware store, a ski shop, a German bakery, and a children's clothing store, among the 20 stores.   Green Mountain Coffee Roasters and Mad River Canoe across the parking lot were fairly new, hoping to expand their market.

Next to my upstairs space was Green Mountain Leather, manufacturing leather clothing and bags. Down the hall was a small antique and resale clothing shop. We had signs on the outside of the building, next to the door leading upstairs. Traffic at the shopping center was very good. I established retail hours from 10 to 4, during the week and 10-2 Saturdays.

Gary, of Green Mountain Leather, had a 'jobber' – salesman - calling on his business accounts and also getting new ones. John, the salesman. volunteered to also represent my bags for a small fee. "It's no extra effort, really. I can carry your portfolio easily along with Gary's," he said.   Indeed, he added several retail outlets throughout New England for me.

Until then I could produce everything myself. Now I needed help and more sewing machines. Trent and I made a quick trip to New York's garment district. "That's where you'll find everything you could possibly need for your business," Gary told me. We found great outlets for the used commercial sewing machines I was looking for. Five machines arrived by truck a week later.

My 20x40 shop served as retail, manufacturing and storage space. Floor to ceiling shelves functioned as dividers. Sewing machines were lined up along the 40-foot long wall, still leaving room for more. The retail display area welcomed customers at the entrance. My cutting table and desk were facing the entrance. I could readily greet all visitors.

The antique shop owner, Rhett, told me that Debbie, her young daughter-in-law was looking for a part-time job. Debbie came to see me one day and I hired her on the spot. She started working for me the day after the machines arrived. Debbie was an experienced seamstress and very conscientious of continuing the quality standards I set.

Debbie and her husband had two young children who just started school. She wanted to use the school hours for work. We set a schedule so that she didn't need to pay anyone for their care. Flex hours were born.

Debbie and others who joined my crew, had a shop key. During the following year I hired four additional seamstresses. They could come in early and leave early. They could also come in after hours if they needed to finish their daily quota. It worked beautifully for all.

The production output increased weekly. I added tote bags with zipper closures, duffle bags, and garment and hockey bags. When specially ordered, I also made huge duffle bags to hold goalie equipment. The children's back-pack I designed became a very popular item. All told I carried 35 different designs. A tag promising a lifetime guarantee was dangling from each bag.

The Sugarbush Ski Area was known as a "Jet-Setter's playground." These affluent visitors loved to shop. Their special orders, with specific color combinations, were a large part of my retail business. I sold the bags in my shop for the same retail prices as the wholesale buyers, so that I was not undermining their sales. Retail mark-up was usually three times the whole sale price.

An executive from Bloomingdales walked in one afternoon. He asked me to design three totes he could take back to New York and present to his retail department heads. They ordered 500 in dark brown with rust trim and an interior zipper pocket for their fall market. The bags had a July delivery date.

I needed more materials and went back to the Howard Bank to ask for a $1,000 loan. It was granted on the spot, no proposal needed. The bank also granted a revolving credit account for the business. It worked like credit cards today. I could withdraw funds and pay back when my accounts paid me.

I bought four additional machines over the phone from the store in New York. Ten machines were all I could fit into the space.

I bought an electric cutting machine. Cutting by hand had become too slow. I hired Cindy, a competent woman, to do all the cutting. Finally I could concentrate on designing, managing and bookkeeping.

By now Jason and Andrea were in junior high school. On the first day of school Andrea walked into home room with a new canvas book bag. "That's a Heidi of Vermont bag!" one of the girls noted.

"Yes, that's my mom."

"Oh, your mother is the bag lady?!" The book bags were very popular. It was evident on days when I was waiting for the children in the school's pick-up lane. More than half of the girls walking out of the school carried one of my totes.

The children stayed interested in my business. One at a time I taught them how to sew on one of those machines. They also came up with advertising slogans, such as 'Wherever you go, keep this bag in tow' meant for a travel tote.

Many years later Jason used his sewing expertise while in the Special Forces. The team had just acquired a 'Foldboat,' a canvas boat with wooden slats that could be folded into a roll. It needed a carrying and storage case. Jason came up with a practical design. The military sent him to LL Bean to oversee its production.

Trent was very proud of how it all turned out. "You know, it gives me some peace knowing that you can create income should anything ever happen to me." I was touched to tears. It never occurred to me that he had these worries as father and husband.

One summer day a part owner of Pappagallo, a women's boutique chain, came upstairs. He had noticed the bags I was hanging downstairs, under the eaves, every morning. "Looks like you can produce volume," he observed. "I have a proposal. Our stores pride themselves with offering one-of-a kind merchandise." I had visited Pappagallo in Burlington often, so I was familiar with the reputation of the store.

"A couple of years ago I saw a unique ladies leather bag that could be done in canvas. Are you a designer?"

"Yes, I have a business degree and designing is part of that education." I didn't tell him that I had to design, cut out the material and produce a ladies bra ready for marketing. "What exactly are you looking for?" I asked.

"The leather bag consisted of the three small pouches, each in a different color. A snap-on wrap-around handle, much like a sling-shot, could be attached to any of the three, creating a different color combination to go with a woman's outfit."

"I can have a sample and price for you in a week," I promised.

Wow! After he left, the women stopped sewing and hooted and hollered! "We'll be busy for a long time. Better find some more seamstresses!"

"First I have to get the order!"

I designed what became the popular *Three-in-one-Tote*. The order came. Pappagallo ordered 6,000 bags. Yes, I would need four additional seamstresses to have nine.

I had ten machines and they were all reliable. Regular maintenance was as simple as a weekly drop of oil at a few key spots. One machine was a spare in case I couldn't fix one. Most break downs were clogged spools, or a broken needle stuck somewhere in the mechanism. Usually I could get the machines working again within a few minutes.

Word spread that I needed seamstresses and I had no trouble hiring. Not everyone was a good fit. But after a few weeks all machines were humming.

One of my new employees was Barbara Von Trapp whom I met on my first evening in Vermont way back in 1964 when she was a young girl. She was the granddaughter of Maria Von Trapp of *The Sound of Music* fame. Barbara was looking for a job that she could manage along with her chores at home. She, along with her unmarried siblings, were living with her parents at their farm. My business neighbor, Gary, suggested that she might want to work for me. Her parents kept a tight rein on their two girls and monitored all activities. They agreed to let Barbara come to town and work for me. Barbara was an experienced sewer, bag after bag was perfect. Along with Debbie, she was the best. It was a good feeling to have reliable employees. It was a congenial group.

I had a sizable stock of canvas in all colors to get started on this humungous order. Six-thousand bags actually translated into 18,000 small bags and 6,000 wrap-around handles.

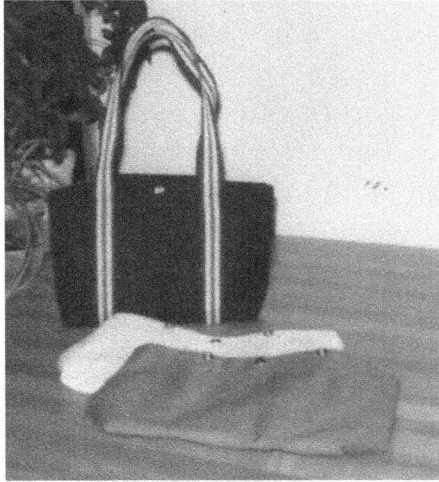

3-in-1 Tote

The color co-ordinated webbing for the handles needed to be specially made. I placed the order immediately. Could we get the webbing fast enough to have the bags ready in time? That was the only unknown.

I estimated that we could have the order completed in four months. My team went to work. They were fast, without compromising the quality that my bags were known for. To keep boredom from setting in, I changed colors every day. Sometimes one woman would sew a complete bag. Other times we had a production line: one sewed the lining, another the canvas bag and a third sewed the lining into the bag. I put in all the snaps that made the bags interchangeable with the wrap-around handle.

Even with a long break over Christmas, because all children were home and moms needed to be there, 6,000 bags were completed by mid February and I started shipping. UPS picked up 120 boxes over a two-week period.

Meanwhile potential customers kept coming upstairs in a steady stream. In the winter it was skiers from all over the world. The Sugarbush Inn hosted many retreats and conferences during the summers. Attendees always found time for shopping. Many buyers turned into repeat customers, often by phone. The quality was a huge selling point.

One of the best testimonials came from Carol May, a woman who'd just returned from a visit to New York City. "Your bags are amazing! I just have to tell you what happened in Manhattan." I motioned to the girls to stop the machines so that they could hear, because they were the ones sewing almost all the bags now.

The room was silent and Carol continued, "I was walking just off Times Square carrying your shoulder bag. Suddenly someone grabbed the bag and tried to run off with it. As he pulled away the shoulder strap slid down my arm and I held onto it. He kept pulling. I held onto the strap with both hands, my feet sliding along the pavement! I figured that the strap would break any second and the thief would get away. But, the strap didn't give! The purse snatcher gave up and ran towards Time Square." We all applauded. She smiled.

"I just had to tell you. This was incredible! I know any other bag would have been ripped apart." We continued talking and the girls later tried to visualize the whole scene.

Some of the most memorable shoppers was a group of several of the Iran hostages who were held for over a year in Teheran and released as President Reagan was sworn in on January 20, 1980. When they walked in, I recognized them immediately. Usually I just let celebrities browse. But this was just a few months after the hostages had returned and I asked one, "Are you Elisabeth Swift?"

"Yes... how do you know me?"

"Your faces were on TV regularly and we were thinking of every one of you the entire time. I just want to welcome all of you back," I said. Elizabeth was one of only two female hostages and her photo was shown most often.

"I'm amazed that, even here in Vermont, I'm being recognized. We had no idea whatsoever about what was going on at home throughout all those months. I'm... we're all very touched by the welcome back."

She continued on that most of the freed hostages had met in Canada for a gathering and were on a side trip to Vermont.

Customers were mesmerized by the production that was going on. Only a few left without buying. From small eyeglass cases to huge duffle bags, I literally offered something for everyone. When people realized they could order a bag in their favorite color combination without an extra charge, they couldn't resist.

I was busier than ever with ordering materials and planning. To keep "my girls" happy, I raised their hourly wage over time as they became more proficient. While at the height of production I instituted two 15-minute breaks in addition to their lunch hour. It was a break from the racket the sewing machines made. Everyone could stretch. They could also talk without having to raise their voices to be heard above the machines.

I was working 10 and 12-hour days and occasionally longer. I went home as usual to make dinner and sit down with Trent and the children. Trent was working weekends, so he was home two days during the week. For those days I cooked a stew or spaghetti sauce in advance on Sundays. Having dinner ready would take less time and I could stay at the shop longer. After dinner I drove back to the shop for a couple of hours. Luckily the shop was only a seven-mile drive away.

Cooking was my balance. No matter how busy or tired I was, standing at the stove, stirring a sauce, was my therapy. Trent sometimes said, "Why don't you just make a hamburger. It is so quick?"

"There's no satisfaction in that," I would answer.

My other sanity check was running. A couple years after starting my business I discovered the sport and became a convert. At first I tried running after getting home, before starting dinner. More and more events would get in the way of that plan and I often did not run at all. Running was important enough for me to get up earlier in the morning and run before heading to the shop. It worked. I didn't miss any runs. This was my time, my problem-solving outing, getting me ready for a busy day.

I kept the weekends free to be at home when Trent was working. One of my workers would be at the shop on Saturdays to be open for retail customers. The business was closed on Sundays.

If I had to be at the shop on Saturdays, I took the children along. They liked the freedom to explore the shopping center on their own. Lunch from the German bakery on the ground floor became our Saturday routine. Their baker made delicious soups every day. Soup and a freshly baked roll was our usual treat.

Although it sounded very impressive to have Bloomingdales and Pappagallo as accounts, businesswise it turned out not to be so. Being profitable became such a fine line that I began questioning the expansion and work needed to keep up.

I remember one discussion very clearly Trent and I had one evening. "I can't see myself keeping up with this year after year," I said to Trent. We had discussed the cut-throat negotiation with the wholesale buyers and my slim bottom line profit for all the effort. After talking back and forth a while, Trent said, "You can fill the orders you have and then slowly phase out one account after the other. Get back to the small business you started."

"But what about all the girls?" I wondered.

"Let them know what is going on. They can find other work over time."

Luckily retailers never returned an item due to poor workmanship. Still, it was extremely challenging to stay in the black. When a big store placed their next order, they were asking for a cut in wholesale price. Meanwhile canvas and other material prices had gone up.

I took one more order from Bloomingdales. Then, with their next order they wanted another price reduction. The buyer said, "I hope you'll agree because we can get it at our price elsewhere."

"Go ahead," I said "At this price I will be in the red, even if everything goes smoothly and no price hikes occur."

Pappagallo reordered because the bags sold fast. Although my costs had gone up, I sold to them at the same price. Sure enough, when they wanted to place a big order with different colors, they asked for a significantly lower wholesale price. I gave up a little, but could still make some profit. This latest Pappagallo order was placed so early that production could be spread out over more months, requiring fewer seamstresses. I told the women that I would be cutting out four positions. "You can continue working here until you find another job," I promised. Four found other work within a couple of weeks. A good core remained.

Once the Pappagallo job was shipped, I gathered the women after a break, "I'm now going to phase out all whole sale accounts during the coming twelve months. It is costing more after all expenses than it brings in."

One of the women, the last one hired by me, laughed sarcastically, "You just wanna get rich and don't give a damn about us." I was not completely surprised by her remark. For a couple of months I had heard some negative drivel from her as I walked into the shop. "Better job...dragon lady..." were some of the phrases I caught. The talk would stop abruptly when she looked up and saw me.

"Please step into the hall with me so that we can continue this conversation." Once outside I asked her if she really meant what she was saying.

"Sure, you business people are all alike."

"All right," I said. "If this is such a bad place to work, don't bother going back to the machine. You can pick up your check tomorrow." She just laughed, picked up her jacket and car keys and was gone.

This experience stung a bit. I thought I treated the women fairly and was a considerate employer.

Barbara left to get ready for her impending marriage. I was really happy for her. She is a good person and I hoped that she would be happy. Trent and I along with the children were invited to her wedding. Over the years we had met all the Von Trapps living in the valley. At the wedding we also met Maria Von Trapp. Until then, Trent and I had seen her at The Trapp Family Lodge, but never actually met. But we heard many stories about her.

She was an elderly woman now and we explained to our trio that she was a grandmother, like Oma, and that she did not resemble the Maria from the movie at all. She wore a festive, traditional Austrian dirndl and was relaxed and smiling at the reception.

I bought an electric monogramming machine that turned into a great business boost. Monograms were popular. Often it was the monogramming that made people buy. Retail sales doubled.

Then my best and most loyal employee left to join the Army. I took it as a signal to speed up my downsizing.

Debbie was divorcing her husband and had two children to raise. She was looking for a new start. I thought she was very brave, but was sad to have her leave at the same time. She left her two children with her mother-in-law until they could live with her. We stayed in touch. After boot-camp she applied for mechanics school. She graduated at the top of her class and stood out among her all-male peers. It didn't surprise me, as I knew she was competent. I was proud to follow her progress. She was accepted to flight school. Eventually she became a top helicopter pilot.

With my encouragement, all but one of the women found other work within a few months. Just like many years before, I could manage the shop and fill mail orders with one employee. Her five-day workweek included Saturdays and I had my weekends. Life moved at a saner pace.

In February of 1984, I had unexpected surgery to remove a diseased kidney. While getting ready for surgery and also after, I often heard "at your age." "....At your age most people with this condition come here in a coma.... At your age, recovery will be slow..." I was 42. That was old in medical circles. I spent two weeks in the hospital with a lot of time to think.

After ten years, the business was routine now and I was wondering what else might be out there for me to discover "at my age." I decided to sell the business.

Real estate agents told me that it would be difficult to sell such a specialized business. They would keep it in mind, however, should anyone make inquiries.

I placed a for-sale ad in the classified section of the *Boston Globe*. The day the ad appeared I received a long distance phone call. "I just saw your ad. Tell me what it entails." I rattled off inventory, machinery and patterns of my designs.

"I have a manufacturing business and from what you're telling me, I think I can incorporate everything. I'm driving up from Boston tomorrow morning. If all is as you say, you have a sale. Will you hold it for me until then?"

"Of course. I'll see you tomorrow." My heart was pounding. Could it be so simple to sell?

The following day John climbed up the stairs to the shop at 11a.m. He surveyed the inventory, tested the machines and agreed to my asking price - no hassling. By 11:30 we had a deal.

He was pleased and I was elated! With all responsibilities of the business lifted, I was ready for whatever was coming my way.

◆◆◆

Hockey Mom

I was introduced to ice hockey at an arena in Basel, where I often skated with friends in the evening. After the public skating session, hockey teams had their turn. We usually watched the game from the adjacent, comfortably warm restaurant. "This is exciting," I was thinking, as the display of speed and skill unfolded. Because it was always getting late, we never watched the entire game, but I would have liked to see a whole game.

Trent and I were skiers when we married in Vermont in 1965. During our first winter together I learned, to my delight, that he was also an accomplished ice hockey player. He'd been skating since he could walk and played ice hockey in prep school. He organized a hockey squad at the University of Connecticut when he found out that the college didn't have one.

Sugarbush Valley's newcomers included many hockey enthusiasts wanting to play. An informal men's league with players from the surrounding towns came to life. They played twice weekly matches at Norwich University's arena at 9 or 10 at night. I couldn't watch those, because it would have meant getting a babysitter - if there was one willing to babysit at these late hours. Trent went alone and verbally replayed the game for me the following morning.

I was learning about the positions: center, forward, defense and goalie. Trent also explained the different plays and how to check or stop an opponent and why players get penalties. For me, knowing what was played out on the ice made the game even more interesting to watch.

Sunday scrimmages were organized at temporary outdoor rinks in the afternoons. Those Sunday games turned into family outings. First we just had Jason to bundle up for a couple of hours. As the family grew, we all went to watch Trent and many of our friends. Between periods our small tykes scrambled onto the ice for some quick laps. Then they scurried off to continue watching with us, just for a few minutes. Quickly they focused their attention on the huge snow pile that grew every week beside the rink due to snow from the Zamboni machine. Once they started sliding down the pile, there was no stopping them.

The men's league continually worked on temporary outdoor ice venues. First, they created a rink in Warren. Later, local gentlemen farmer Steve Flemr donated enough of his farmland in the center of Waitsfield to build a regulation ice surface. But, of course, being outdoors, the season was short, even in Vermont's cold winters. When the ice got too soft for skating, the players had to travel to the Norwich arena again.

It was only natural that Jason, Andrea and Derek also wanted to skate and play hockey. And that was the beginning of what turned into eighteen winters spent in cold ice rinks - no more watching from a cozy, warm restaurant! Hockey Mom was my new title. Ice hockey turned into our family's winter sport. Our lives evolved around hockey; I was a happy participant. Having a common interest certainly kept the family together during the children's teenage years.

Jason was the first to participate in the loosely organized skating group that evolved into a Youth Hockey League - YHL. All age levels were coached by hockey player dads. Andrea and Derek followed when they could skate around a rink without falling. Our YHL organized scrimmages and games with others in towns within a forty-mile radius. Car-pooling became a welcomed component.

Ice hockey was a fairly new, not widely followed sport, in the United States. It was really Canada's national sport. We were in ski country. Sugarbush and Stowe were a mecca for skiers. Our fledgling skaters were few. Parents made it happen. Without parents organizing, driving and at times shoveling the rink, hockey would not have grown in our area.

Three different jerseys – three different teams

Our three children were on the same team only once in the beginning; then on two different ones and eventually three. Carpooling did not cover the spread of our involvement and both Trent and I were usually on the road. Twice during the week for practices and then Sunday morning games. Being a realtor, Trent was working on Sundays. Hockey Mom was the carpool driver.

During those years I perfected my cook-ahead and reheat dishes. Sunday afternoons became long cooking sessions. The children got caught up on homework, played games, or had some quiet time curled up in front of the fireplace with a book. One at a time they kept me company. Sitting on the kitchen counter we would rehash their hockey game as I chopped and stirred. Whatever I prepared for dinner that day, I doubled the recipe for another meal. At the same time I may have made a chili con carne and a vegetable stew. I baked a chicken and meatloaf simultaneously. Those dishes would see us through the week when Trent and I were working with no time to cook.

In addition to taking our skaters to various ice rinks, Trent created home ice on the only level area of our lawn. It was simple to maintain in the very cold Vermont winters. Removing newly fallen snow was a bigger challenge. But we had three very willing volunteers for that. With brooms and shovel they cleared the ice in no time and were skating. In the summer, a couple of plywood sheets in front of the barn served as ice. There they practiced to hit marks on the imaginary net on the barn wall.

Trent was coaching from the very beginning. First, the young mini-mites and then he graduated to the next level along with the skaters.

When hockey season ended the skaters were looking forward to hockey school. The Vermont Hockey School in Burlington was started by three University of Vermont alumni in 1974. Ted Child, Ted Castle and Will McKinnon rose to local fame, playing and garnering many awards. Their hockey camp was based on having fun and built drills into that environment.

Our first trip to the two-week hockey camp was in mid-July 1975. Derek celebrated his 5th birthday there. The obligatory T-shirt fitted him like a floor-length gown. It just added to the fun. The two-week camp meant a daily, early-morning drive to Burlington. The car was loaded to the max with players and their equipment: helmets, mouth guards, shoulder, elbow and shin pads, padded hockey pants and several hockey sticks per player. No one made a sound during the one-hour drive. They were still half asleep!

Along with hockey equipment I also packed snacks and a lunch. The indoor arena was at the shore of Lake Champlain, perfect for a picnic and swim. I was looking forward to a swim, as much as they did – getting from the winter sport back into summer.

The drive home was much livelier. Energized from that refreshing dip in the lake, the skating sessions were glowingly rehashed, "Did you see me speeding by Pat. Wow, I was fast today!" And so it went all the way home.

Andrea quickly turned into a speedy and fearless hockey player. When she was ten, she decided to stop because she no longer wanted to be the only girl. She really was becoming a skilled player, but there was no persuading her to continue.

After several years of going to the Vermont Hockey School camp, Jason and Derek went to other summer schools for even more experience; Jason for defense and Derek as goalie. Hockey Mom traveled to camps all over New England. When the boys went to hockey camp, Trent headed to coaching clinics.

It never entered my mind that the boys could get hurt. We bought quality hockey equipment and then I kept my fingers crossed that their bodies and teeth would be protected. During all those years of hockey, injuries were few.

When Derek was varsity goalie, he did get hit. It happened during an out-of-town game, one of the few that I did not attend. I'm actually glad that I didn't see the puck that zoomed straight towards his head. The helmet broke in half. Derek didn't get a concussion, but he had 12 stitches decorating his forehead. It did not keep him from manning the goal at the next game.

Trent was knocked off his feet once while coaching when a player lost control. He bumped hard into Trent and before he knew it, Trent was flat on his back. He didn't wear a helmet and hit his head hard. I held my breath until I saw him get up and knew he was all right. After that incident Trent wore a helmet any time he was on the ice. I was always relieved when practices and games were completed without injuries.

With school and sport activities filling our days, we didn't watch much television. National Hockey League

(NHL) games were the exception, even before the children were actively playing. Luckily we lived close to the Canadian border and could watch games as they were broadcast by the Canadian channels. U.S. stations only covered special events. Our family's loyalties were divided between the Boston Bruins and the Montreal Canadians. Bobby Orr of Boston and Guy LaFleur of Montreal were at the height of their game. We followed them closely and we rarely missed any matches.

So, when the 1980 Olympic Games in Lake Placid came around, we were solid and knowledgeable ice hockey fans. With bowls of freshly made popcorn, we crowded in front of the TV set for all Olympic hockey games that were broadcast. Every time team USA advanced we were almost as excited as the players. When the team reached the semi-finals, our excitement jumped up a notch. They had to play the Soviet Union National Team.

The Russians had ruled Olympic hockey and were the favorites. It was a fact that the Russians were seasoned professional players. Our squad consisted of college boys from different areas, together just for the Olympic Games. The two teams played an exhibition game two weeks before the Olympics - the Russians won by 10 goals.

The semi-final match was played on a Friday night. We huddled in front of the TV set as usual. The Russians scored first. It was a very low scoring game, no one left the room so as not to miss any seconds of play. We were cheering or groaning constantly, depending on what was happenings on the ice. Half-way through the final period our team was ahead by one goal, 4-3. Those last ten minutes crept by very slowly.

During the closing seconds ABC's announcer, Al Michaels, yelled, "11 seconds, ten seconds... Do you believe in miracles?" And finally, "Yesssssssss!"

The U.S. team won to advance to the gold medal round. We beat the experienced Soviet's team. Unheard of!

We could not believe what we had just witnessed! This game is now known as the "Miracle on Ice." It became the number one ice hockey story of the century.

The United States squad won the next game also and with it, the gold medal. But it is the game against the Soviets that lingers in our memory.

Ice hockey had arrived in the United States at last!

Jason and Derek went to their practices and games with new vigor. They were always ready to get into the car. I never had to nag - not once. I could almost see the Olympic symbol twirling in their heads.

Now, ice hockey was a growing sport all across the country and Vermont as well. In 1982, the YHL board members petitioned the Harwood school board to accept ice hockey as a varsity sport. They agreed under the condition that the league cover all expenses. Trent was hired to coach our high school's first varsity hockey team. Jason became a member of the varsity squad. Andrea had stayed involved. She often came along with me to watch games. Now she was keeping statistics for the new team.

In addition to Hockey Mom, I was now also the coach's wife. Watching games with other parents became a different experience from when the skaters were younger. Now it was VARSITY!

I enjoyed watching Jason's progress and contributions towards the varsity team. He was a quick and shifty defenseman. He skated smoothly and fast. He could change direction instantly and often surprised opponents by skating by them untouched.

At the same time I also had to listen to the crowds opinions of the coach's actions. "Now - why did he send Tim out? He can't play defense!" I didn't pass any critiques on to Trent as he had plenty to think about when he was preparing for the next practice or game.

Sometimes, the small team barely had enough players to be competitive. The boys were dedicated, worked hard and the ones on the bench egged on the group that was on the ice. As a new team they were the underdogs. Against all odds they were victorious three times during that first winter. It was very satisfying to be at all the games, knowing that support from the bleachers made a difference to the players. They truly never gave up - no matter the score. Their record improved every season. I still loved watching the game.

Jason graduated after the team's first season. He was accepted at West Point Military Academy. He hoped to play hockey there also, but did not make the team. Jason was crushed and it put him in a slump. Suddenly he couldn't participate in the sport that he grew up with. After Trent had a conversation with the guidance counselor, West Point made a rare exception for a plebe (freshman). They allowed Jason to play off campus with the local men's team. It made all the difference to Jason and also to me. Trent and I knew that being able to continue playing hockey would lift his sense of self.

Derek was goalie for most of his hockey playing days. I believe this is the most difficult kind of Hockey Mom to be. When the team is winning, parents don't pay any attention to the goalie. When they are on the losing side, it is the goalie's fault, naturally. We had many long drives home where Derek could vent, which he never did on the ice or in the locker room. I listened. I was very conscious of supporting Derek while not criticizing the coach, whoever it was. When Derek became varsity goalie, we were at the same arena at last; Derek and Trent with the team and me watching from the bleachers.

During some hotly contested matches it was a big challenge not to react to other parents' enthused comments. They were very vocal and didn't hold back. "Derek should have stopped that puck; he could see it coming from a mile away!" Or, "Trent sure has his favorites. He just doesn't play Bob. I'm gonna complain to the A.D." That it might have to do with ability, specially playing a very experienced team, didn't matter. I had to bite my tongue many times.

Those comments really upset me, because I knew he was a very sharp and athletic goalie. It wasn't just Hockey Mom's opinion. In a game against the elite Barre High School team, 87 shots were fired at Derek. In a losing effort, he stopped 82 of those shots. After the game, several parents from the Barre team approached coach Trent, "Who is your goalie? That's the best performance I've ever seen."

After six years as varsity coach, Trent resigned when Derek graduated in 1988. No more Hockey Mom watching at cold ice rinks. I didn't miss it one bit.

We moved to coastal North Carolina in the mid 1990s and found that ice hockey had spread even to the South. Wilmington had just opened a new indoor skating rink, complete with an adjoining, heated cafeteria. It didn't take long for players of all ages to find one another.

Derek, who also lived in Wilmington with his family, joined the men's league. Trent, playing defense, skated with the 40-and-over senior team. The league grew with amateur skaters, as well as semi-pro players.

After several years Wilmington sported enough teams to have a season ending championship. There was a shortage of goalies. The senior team recruited Derek, although he was not yet 40. It was allowed since other squads in the league also had 'under-age' goalies.

Finally Trent and Derek were playing together. No longer the Hockey Mom with responsibilities, I enjoyed following the action from a cozy vantage point. If I didn't feel like getting cold feet, I abandoned the bleachers for the warm cafeteria. I could see the entire arena from the ceiling-high Plexiglas windows and, sitting on a comfy chair, happily watched all games from there.

In 2005, Wilmington's senior team won the play-offs. Trent and Derek were hockey champs.

Better than Christmas

———•—•—

Before Trent and I married in 1965, I heard many immigrants bemoan what they were missing from the old country. They seemed to be living more in the past. I was determined not to do that and immersed myself in all American customs and traditions.

I learned to appreciate Thanksgiving, Valentine's Day, and Halloween, celebrations that were not known in Germany. However, at Christmastime, my favorite holiday with the fondest memories, I stuck by my German traditions.

Trent went along and embraced my German Christmas, including the Advent's wreath, an Advent calendar and the Christmas Eve gift giving instead of on Christmas Day.

I made an Advent's wreath with fir and pine boughs to hold candles – one each of the four Sundays before Christmas. On Sunday afternoons, when evening was approaching, we had hot chocolate and a few cookies in the living room. Then I lit the appropriate number of candles on the wreath and we talked about our Christmas wishes.

The Advent calendar was the other countdown to Christmas. On December 1, we opened a tab on the calendar, revealing a seasonal picture like an angel or a candle. A new tab was opened daily until December 24. Christmas had arrived!

Trent and I set up the tree only days before in the living room. Instead of electric lights we placed candles amidst the multi-colored glass ornaments. My mother had sent a box of metal candle-holder clips from Germany that securely held the candles on the branches. Presents that had arrived by mail were placed under the tree.

We lived in rural Vermont where snow usually covers the countryside by Thanksgiving. On Christmas Eve, the children busied themselves quietly in their rooms upstairs from afternoon onwards, knowing that Santa was arriving soon. Because we didn't have a fireplace and chimney, Santa always parked his sled on our driveway. With the children safely out of sight, Santa scattered his presents around the tree and then hurried to the next house.

After six o'clock, when it was dark, we lit the candles on the tree and turned off all other lights. I played a record with traditional German Christmas carols sung softly by a children's choir. Then Trent rang a bell signaling that Santa arrived.

We gathered Jason, Andrea and Derek outside the living room door and went in together. Only the warm candlelight from the tree illuminated the room, casting soft shadows. The fresh greens of the tree filled the air with a woodsy aroma. The tree reminded me of my early childhood Christmases in the 1940s in Berlin, when the tree often was the only present. It still brought back the same warm, fuzzy feelings I felt then.

The children were happy to see the tree in it's holiday dress, topped with a large angel. When they were aware enough, they worried that the tree might catch fire. But I showed them how the candles were carefully placed and not close to the branches above. We also never let the candles burn when no one was in the room.

We settled around the tree and Trent handed out the presents, one at a time. Some were from Santa, others from Grancy, Trent's mother and from Oma, as my mother was known. In between we paused for a traditional

German Christmas Eve supper: potato salad that I made in the morning, German sausage and crunchy rolls.

When all presents were opened amid squeals of delight, "Oh, I was really wishing for it!" we admired each other's gifts. We complemented Santa for bringing the perfect toy, book or game. After the pile of crumpled wrapping paper was cleared, Trent and I relaxed. We slept in Christmas Day morning, while the children continued with toys and games where they left off the evening before.

Christmas breakfast concluded with a slice of traditional Christmas stollen. It is similar to fruitcake, but much lighter, more like a scone than cake. There was no family around to visit. Our day was spent sledding or skating and then everyone would curl up with their favorite book or game until dinner, while I put a leg of lamb in the oven. This was my mother's Christmas roast of choice and I made it our traditional dinner also, even before we were raising sheep.

So, what could be better than this?

Oma's visits every July.

Oma spent Christmas with us only once. It was in 1969, one of the coldest and snowiest winters in Vermont. Bundled up in a dark brown beaver coat that made her four-foot and a half figure look like a little bouncing ball from a distance, we went for our daily walk. Flanked by over five-foot snow banks, she wowed, "I'm not coming back in the winter! How do you manage year after year?"

I assured her, "It really isn't like this every winter." I know she didn't believe me.

True to her words, Oma only came in the summer. She was working at Osram, the world's largest manufacturer of light bulbs and electronics. She started out on the assembly line. Her knack for intricate, detailed work brought her to the team that developed new products like LED lighting. This meant higher wages and added pride in her work. Most businesses in Germany close for vacations in July and August, which made it possible for her to stay with us for four weeks, sometimes even six.

Oma's arrival was anticipated as much as Christmas. One memorable visit happened when our children were eight, six and four. It started with meeting her at the airport. We couldn't all fit into our small aqua blue Subaru station wagon. Who would be able to come with me? This time Jason was the one. Trent stayed at home with the other two, anxiously awaiting our return. Sometimes I only had to drive to the Burlington airport, 45 minutes from our house. More often though, her economy flights would land in Montreal, a six- hour round trip.

I was looking forward to having my mother close by. She didn't have a telephone until the mid-1970s. All communication and arrangements were by mail. I sent a weekly letter, keeping her up-to-date about our lives like, "Trent finished sheet rocking the baby's room." News about the children usually was the main topic, "Andrea fell off her tricycle, but except for two scraped knees she is fine." The only time we could actually talk was during my mother's visits.

At the airport Jason and I were eagerly watching every passenger emerging from the plane. Finally Oma appeared at the door. "I see her!" Jason was jumping up and down. Oma looked up and waved, knowing we were somewhere behind that row of floor-to-ceiling windows in the arrival building. She always carried two large shopping bags, her purse and a coat.

The time until she was passed customs was moving at a snail's pace. "How much longer?" Jason kept asking.

I didn't know but answered, "Oh, she'll be done any minute." Finally we spotted her suitcase decorated with colorful tape and decals on a cart moving towards us, followed by a tired-looking but smiling Oma. After we each embraced her tightly, I took her suitcase and Jason attached himself to Oma's side. He was talking non-stop,

Oma nodded and smiled. She didn't speak English but always seemed to get the gist.

On the drive home, my mother was sitting in the front and Jason in back. He positioned himself in the middle so that he could hold Oma's hand through the gap between seats. Once on the road, my mother relayed all the news about the neighbors, our neighborhood and the relatives in Berlin. By the time I pulled into our driveway, all was said and she could focus totally on the greeting committee of Trent, Andrea and Derek. "*Ach, wie gut Euch zu sehen,*" – it's so good to see you, hugging every one again and again.

When Trent wanted to take her suitcase upstairs, where she shared the room with Andrea, she said, "*Nein –* I have things in it for you.*" He left it in the living room. After a few minutes of refreshing herself, she motioned us, "*Komm,*" – come here.

Oma kneeled on the rug in front of the sofa and opened her suitcase. We could see it was full of clothes, but not hers. Her neighbors had been saving their grandchildren's outgrown clothes and gave them to Oma. These hand-me-downs looked almost brand new, not a worn spot in sight. Oma handed a couple of dresses to Andrea, fake brown leather pants to Jason and Derek, tops and even a winter coat for Andrea and parkas for the boys. Miraculously, everything fit our gang of three, who immediately put on an impromptu fashion show for us.

Between the clothes, she had tucked many different foods that were still hard to get in rural Vermont: Cold cuts like thinly sliced Black Forest ham; prosciutto; chunks of smoked bacon; veal and pork sausages, all vacuum sealed, so there was no give-away odor.

Derek, Andrea and Jason's eyes were getting wider and wider as Oma proceeded. Her suitcase was like a magician's top hat; she pulled out pumpernickel bread, bags of Gummi Bears – the children's favorite German candy - and many chocolate bars. Everyone could pick a favorite. Mine always was dark chocolate laden with whole hazelnuts. Finally, a few of her dresses and shoes were all that was left in the suitcase.

Then Oma picked up her coat that was draped on the sofa. With an "I have a secret" smile lighting up her round face, she produced four bottles of German white wine from the sleeves, Trent's favorites. She had sewn the sleeves shut and carried the wine right passed customs without paying extra Duty. She was extremely proud of her smuggling prowess. I can imagine how she enjoyed plotting and executing her smuggling plan to pull off this surprise!

In the shopping bags she had a few board games. They would be set up on the kitchen table, keeping her and the children amused for hours during the coming weeks.

"Wow! This is like Christmas - only better!" Derek said.

"Really?" Trent asked.

"Yeah!! Because we got Oma too!"

With Oma

♦♦♦

One Ticket – Two Tickets

The sound of opera was a welcome presence in our apartment as I was growing up. We only had a radio for entertainment, but stations played music from all genres throughout the day. On Sundays it was usually all classical, including opera.

Mutti was an opera lover and usually commented about an opera's storyline. I loved the music more than the stories. I found opera very soothing - it nurtured my soul. When I listened to the music, I no longer noticed the cloudy, cold day and the rubble outside.

In 1957, when I was fifteen, I went to the Deutsche Oper in Berlin for my first live performance. Like everyone I had one black dress for special occasions, which I wore to the opera. Mutti, who couldn't afford a second ticket, recited what I could expect: checking my coat; walking around to stretch my legs during the two intermissions; walking slowly and eavesdropping on people's conversations.

As I made my way to the opera house, I could tell who was also going there by their formal dress. Everyone, from parquet to fifth balcony patrons, was dressed in their best, as was tradition. I got goose bumps entering the vast hall. I felt very comfortable in the hushed atmosphere and couldn't wait for the curtain to go up. I'm not sure where exactly I was sitting but I do remember that I could see and hear perfectly. Berlin always attracted the finest talent, and the performance of The Flying Dutchman by Richard Wagner was no different. World-renowned tenor, Lauritz Melchior, was one of the stars.

The three acts flew by and although the score was a bit heavier than some other operas that I liked, I was mesmerized and would have loved for it to go on longer. As everyone was leaving, conversations were more animated. People were smiling.

Mutti waited for me outside. It was almost midnight, and she didn't like the thought of me going home alone. During the short bus ride home, she wanted to get a complete report about the singers, the set, and so on. After that performance I loved the music even more and went to the opera often, wherever I lived. New York City was an especially exciting place to be. Opera offerings covered a wide scope from expected traditional favorites to some not often performed.

While I had my canvas bag business, I went to Manhattan every fall. I made sure that the opera season had begun. On those trips I packed in visits to suppliers; a running race; and a musical and opera for fun.

In 1980, the Metropolitan Opera musicians were on strike. No opera. But I had a ticket for the musical *Evita* for Friday evening. I was really happy that I would be able to see the always sold out performances and was looking forward to the evening.

On that morning I took the bus to Rockefeller Center for a visit to Barnes & Noble, where I usually spent a couple of hours. I noticed a short line outside one of the B&N's entrances. "What is happening?" I asked a well-dressed woman standing in line.

"Pavarotti is going to sign his newest record. Do you like opera?"

"I sure do and especially Pavarotti. When is this going to start?"

"One o'clock."

There was no decision to make. I joined the line. It was shortly before noon and the November weather was actually pleasant. I was number ten in the line that quickly grew during the following hour. I was amazed at my timing; arriving at B&N when Pavarotti was going to be there. I had seen him at the Metropolitan, but never imagined I would meet him in person.

Soon B&N personnel were outside for crowd control. I learned that Luciano Pavarotti was booked to sing two operas and was in Manhattan for the duration, hoping the strike would end. Meanwhile his new recording of arias was just released and the signing was scheduled from 1 to 3p.m.

Just before one it was announced that Mr. Pavarotti would be a little late. The staff handed out bottles of water. Then they came around with huge Pavarotti buttons to keep us entertained. Shortly after, the first ten people were ushered inside. It was my luck to be included. Being the last in the group gave me time to watch the proceedings.

As we entered, Pavarotti's glorious tenor was heard over the sound system. Everyone was listening, creating a calm atmosphere. He was seated at a table in an elevated section of the store. Even from a distance he looked much larger than I remembered from his performance on stage.

Our group was lined up at the step leading to his table after purchasing the record. I watched as Pavarotti nodded to the man in charge of letting people approach his table. A woman quickly walked up the three steps. Pavarotti gave his broadest smile as she handed the record cover over for his signature. I couldn't hear, but they were obviously chatting. He never broke eye contact.

I was getting nervous, trying to rehearse a few words to say. What could I say? He probably heard every compliment hundreds of times. Some people had longer conversations with the singer than others. During one conversation with a fan, one of the staff approached the table. Pavarotti just stretched an arm in his direction with a stop motion while staying totally focused on the fan. After their conversation he turned to the staff.

Finally it was my turn. I was gliding up the steps to the table. He smiled, "Bongiorno! What is your name please?"

"Heidi Smith," I said.

He nodded and while he was writing his dedication I babbled something like "I'm so happy to meet you. I heard you in Aida and have many of your records. Your voice is just wonderful!"

He nodded "Thank you, I am sorry that I cannot sing at the Metropolitan this time," and handed the record back to me and shook my hand. "Thank you for coming and buying my record."

That was it. I floated out of the store and kept looking at the record cover he just had signed, making sure it was real.

On my way to *Evita*, I had to get off at the B&N bus stop. It was 7p.m. and a long line was outside the store. I wondered what else might be going on. An employee told me, "Pavarotti is still signing autographs. He promised the crowd he'll stay until the last one is gone." I was impressed and admired Pavarotti the person even more.

As our children grew up, Mutti visited in the early fall instead of during summer vacation. I tried to take her to an opera in New York often. Two of those visits were especially memorable.

Trent's cousin, William Parcher, a baritone, was performing at the New York City Opera during several seasons. I bought a couple of tickets for The Ballad of Baby Doe, where Bill was singing. Mutti always liked to go to New York. I called Bill, told him when we would be attending and he said, "If you have not been backstage, I'll give you a tour afterwards." The prospect of a backstage tour made this opera outing even more exciting.

We were not familiar with the opera. But it was always a treat to be at a live performance and we enjoyed becoming familiar with another opera.

As promised, Bill was at the stage door after the performance and greeted us. It was actually quite noisy inside. With their job done, everyone was relaxing. Singers and crew were in animated conversations in the huge, stark room.

We made our way around canvas backdrops, suspended from the ceiling that was so high that I couldn't see the top. Ropes were dangling down all around us. Bill was giving explanations of how backdrops were changed, often in record time, and I translated all for Mutti. She had never been backstage, and she kept listening and nodding. Mutti was at least a foot shorter than I, and had to tilt her had way back to see everything Bill was pointing to. She talked about her backstage visit for years.

As far back as I can recall, *The Pearl Fishers* by George Bizet was Mutti's all-time favorite opera. Although very popular, it was rarely performed. In the late 1980s I spotted the opera in the line-up at the New York City Opera. I immediately reserved two tickets for a Sunday matinee in late September. Then I called Mutti, who was still in Berlin, "We have tickets for your favorite opera in September!"

She was surprised, "I don't believe it. Oh, I can't wait." My usually matter-of-fact mother was quite animated. I was excited too, as we would have a fabulous outing.

Beverly Sills, retired American soprano superstar, became director of the New York City Opera at Lincoln Center in 1980. It had been teetering on the verge of bankruptcy for several years. I had read that she was working long hours, seven days a week, to make the company solvent. One of her innovations was producing rarely performed operas. They always sold out quickly. Slowly she was able to put the opera house's finances solidly in the black.

I planned to make our opera excursion a day trip. Peoples Express airline was offering incredibly low priced flights to New York. On a clear and calm Sunday morning we left Burlington at 8 a.m. and by 10:30 we were strolling down Fifth Avenue.

It was eerily quiet in the city. Sometimes we were standing in the middle of the avenue to look up at the skyscrapers without honking cars rushing by. We window shopped all the way and arrived at Lincoln Center in plenty of time. We rested on the edge of the fountain in the middle of the plaza until it was time to go in.

We quickly found our seats in the parquet section. Mutti looked around and spotted Beverly Sills on a side balcony above us. "I'm sure the singers know that she's here. I bet they'll try their best. We're in for a treat." Mutti was convinced.

Every seat was taken by the time the curtain rose and the familiar overture began. Mutti was right. The orchestra and singers were in top form. While we were sipping a glass of champagne during the intermission, we recalled the first act and couldn't find fault.

People watching was interesting too. Opera dress code was more relaxed now, especially at matinees. Mutti was shaking her head when a woman in blue jeans and casual blouse walked by, "That's terrible. What's the world coming to?!"

The music transported us through the rest of the opera. Finally the lights went on and after many curtain calls, it was time to leave.

Our stomachs were growling by now and we headed to a little Italian restaurant nearby. During the leisurely early dinner we went over the performances again and again. The performance was as good as any recording we had listened to. We declared to be the luckiest people to have finally seen this opera. We were back at LaGuardia airport in plenty of time for our 8p.m. return trip.

I was all wound up and thought about writing Beverly Sills to thank her for providing the impetus for this once-in-a-lifetime experience with my mother.

Then I remembered reading her biography. As a young singer Beverly spent time in Berlin. She liked the opera house, but not the city. She was Jewish and resented everything Berlin represented in recent history. I kept thinking, "I shouldn't write. She probably doesn't want to hear from a German and especially one from Berlin."

Monday morning I wrote my note anyway. I quickly recited how my mother, living in Berlin, always wanted to see the opera; that we 'People Expressed' ourselves to New York for the day; how special the performance was. I thanked her for staging it and to please give our admiration to the singers. I mailed the letter that afternoon so that I couldn't change my mind.

Friday's mail packet was especially thick. As I pulled it out of the mailbox by the side of the road, a postcard fell to the ground. The card was from the New York City Opera. I quickly turned it over.

> "Dear Ms. Smith,
> What a nice letter and thanks
> for taking the time to write.
>> Sincerely,
>> Beverly Sills."

This busy woman was thanking me for taking the time to write! I was awestruck!

To this day, whenever any personal mail arrives, I answer by return mail.

◆◆◆

Coach

"You're not a coach!" A five-year-old aspiring ice hockey player looked at me from a group of 15 or so. Some in the group nodded in agreement.

"No," I said, "but I'll try." Our breaths created white mist in the cold evening air.

It was early January in Montpelier, Vermont, and already dark with temperatures hovering in the single digits. Trent and I had driven the 20 miles to the hockey rink for one of the weekly 5:30 p.m. practices of the Youth Hockey League. The coach for the 5 & 6 year olds didn't show. Derek was in this group.

Only a few parents were standing by the rink. Trent was coaching the older group that included Jason and Andrea. He was already on the ice at one half of the arena. I was elected to keep these youngsters busy for 45 minutes.

As I had watched their coach do at many practices, I kept them racing each other, jumping over hockey sticks and playing tag the entire time. Not another peep from the group. Luckily I didn't have to do it again.

The offer to really coach came unexpectedly years later. Trent and I were running regularly with the high school cross-country team at their training sessions. In the spring, we also helped with track and field events. Jason and Andrea were part of both teams.

After several seasons the coach, John Kerrigan, invited Trent to join the coaching team. "I wish I could, but right now I travel often, come home late and work every weekend. I couldn't help at the meets at all." After a pause he suggested, "Why not ask Heidi?"

Kerrigan asked me if I would consider coaching the junior high runners. I didn't hesitate, "Yes, of course, I'll be glad to."

The timing was good. I still had my Heidi of Vermont business but could make all the afternoon practices. Varsity and junior high were in the same complex. That made it natural for the teams to train together on the hilly country roads.

John Kerrigan was the high school's biology teacher. He had established great rapport with all students. Kerrigan, as he was universally addressed, an accomplished runner in his mid-thirties, had earned students' respect in this field as well. Slim of stature and endowed with a booming voice, runners at the front of the group could hear, "Pick up the pace, guys!" even when he was bringing up the rear. I knew he would be easy to get along with. I also knew I would be learning much about training and coaching and was excited for the season to get started.

Kerrigan suggested that we encourage elementary students to join our training runs. "If we can get them hooked on running, we could build consistent teams for years to come."

I visited the elementary schools in the surrounding towns to make my recruiting pitch to students just before gym classes. I told them, "We have a lot of fun as a group. You may find you like the after-school runs," and finished with, "You can stop anytime."

Just as we had guessed, the students who responded had siblings at the high school and were familiar with the program. Others were too intimidated by the high school environment. Eventually a few additional 5th and 6th graders did join the group. Kim Blodgett, a tiny, skinny wisp of a 5th grader, was the only one from Moretown. Derek had just entered junior high and there was no question in his mind that he would be a runner. He had already been part of all family running activities. In total we had between 20 to 30 skinny runners at training runs and school meets.

Running is a sport where the coach does not watch from the sidelines. Kerrigan and I were running with the young athletes at every training session. I was usually in the back with the newcomers, giving moral support.

I loved running and could still relate to the days when I wanted to quit after every run. But I didn't and my daily run became a part of my life, like eating and breathing. As the years went by and I reached goals, like lowering my race pace and completing the half-marathon milestone, I became more confident and self-assured.

"Just stop, catch your breath and in a couple of minutes you'll feel ready to finish the run," was one of many quiet encouragements as we shuffled along a dirt road. I hoped the young runners wouldn't quit the team before they had experienced the joy of accomplishing a difficult uphill run.

Varsity runners were also wonderful with the newbies. They were very empathetic, often running long stretches with them. I watched them as they picked up the pace slowly while their chatter was in the air. Other times, especially as they made their way up a hill, their crunching footsteps was the only sound.

With very few exceptions, all school meets were scheduled for Saturdays. Varsity and junior high were held at the same venue, but competed in separate races. Students were testing themselves against runners their age, their true competitors. The 3-mile-race courses were sending runners through woods and over open fields. Parents, coaches and other runners lined the course and cheered on all competitors. "Looking good!" "Keep going!" and "You're almost there!" were enthusiastically shouted until everyone had crossed the finish line.

In cross-country, everyone really runs his or her own race. Yes, they are competing against their peers, but they are really running against their own best times. Some athletes are naturally faster than others. Some are better at short distances; others have the endurance for longer ones. It was interesting to watch students find what best suited them and then, all on their own volition, train to improve. "Maybe next time I can finish ahead of Lisa!"

That's where coaching made a difference. One runner needed to work on more uphill runs, another had to concentrate on short, fast spurts to improve stamina. With specific individual training schedules, runners improved their times. Running in blistering heat and during a snowstorm were bonding experiences. Individuals turned into a team that supported one another. Sparkling eyes, happy smiles and hugs after races were their rewards. I watched as students evolved from timid participants to confident ones. They became ambassadors for running and even went about recruiting new runners every year.

By coaching the junior high team I could be involved with both Derek and Andrea. She was a varsity runner. But since we always practices together I could see her progress firsthand. She became the top varsity girl and was leading the team for four years. Kerrigan, of course, was coaching her. But he asked me to take her to some season ending races out of state that she qualified for. With his instructions echoing in my ears, I took Derek along to cheer Andrea at the New England championship race in Rhode Island.

During the off-season our family went to road races throughout Vermont. We often saw runners from our school and other school teams as well. The sport is a welcoming fraternity with friendly rivalries. With all this training, my running times improved along with the students'. Slowly I whittled my pace from 9 minutes per mile to a race pace of 7 minutes per mile during my favorite annual 4-mile run in Central Park.

Kim, who started running with us as a 5th grader, couldn't wait to get to junior high to be able to compete in races. She always had a cheery disposition, and her sparkling blue eyes reflected her joy of running. She remained tiny and it was quite amusing, seeing her look up at some of the varsity runners and playing cheerleader. Once in high school, she became state champion in our school division twice. She was one of the best runners in the state. I was so happy for her!

Track and field was slightly different. Because of many events to compete in, teams were much larger. There were more coaches to work with the athletes. I was involved with running, the triple jump and long jump. Running I could relate to. Training was very similar to cross-country.

For the jumping events I looked to Kerrigan for advice. I also watched many training videos to learn how to best help the students. I couldn't demonstrate, but I was able to relate that the most important part was the run-up to the take-off board. Great speed build-up would make it possible to explode off the board to achieve maximum distance. With so many events, afternoon practices at the track were noisy and busy. Definitely more draining than training cross-country runners.

Along with the athletes, I was introduced to the endless rules of track and field competition. A runner would be disqualified after a false start or by stepping into the adjacent lane. Putting a toe past the take-off bar for jumping would disallow the jump. There were many more disappointed students than in cross country. Only taking a short-cut would get a runner disqualified.

I also learned that a coach could get a runner disqualified. I was on the track infield cheering Andrea on during a race, when a volunteer at the meet casually strolled up to me and said, "You're not supposed to be here. It is against the rules. You could get the athlete disqualified." Oops. I had no idea. I felt extremely embarrassed and watched my steps from then on.

After I stopped coaching, I followed the athletes' progress during their high school careers and beyond. I kept meeting former students who continued running after graduating at many road races. They were now running for the fun of it; they were hooked for life. I felt that I had made a difference by introducing young boys and girls to running; the sport that gave me confidence and joy.

After 40 years of teaching and coaching, Kerrigan is still at it. So far, he has coached his cross-country teams to 22 state championships.

Andrea and I are still running together occasionally. The most recent race was a half-marathon team event in New York's Central Park.

◆◆◆

III - Ripple Effects

One Kidney

How often do we take a look at our life, asking ourselves: What have I done to this point? Are there things yet to accomplish?

For me the opportunity came when I was spending two weeks in a hospital with plenty of time to take stock.

In the fall of 1983, I came down with severe back pains and a high fever. I had always been healthy except for recurring supposed pneumonias while growing up and occasional bladder infections later on. This back pain and fever seemed familiar; it could be a bladder infection. I wasn't worried. The fever crept higher for several days.

"I don't like this," Trent said. It was a Sunday and he took me to the emergency room in Montpelier. The doctor couldn't find anything except cloudy urine. "Looks like a bladder infection." He wrote a prescription to clear it up, "When this is gone, go to your doctor for a check-up. You should feel better in a few days."

Soon I was well enough to go back to my store and coaching the junior high runners. The medication ran out after three weeks and I made an appointment with Dr. Nowlan, a new young doctor at our local health clinic. He told me, "The infection has not cleared up. Here is a prescription for another round. See me when it's gone."

After three weeks I was back in Dr. Nowlan's office. The urine sample still showed an infection. He said, "Whatever it is should have cleared up by now. I don't like this." He referred me to Dr. Poplowski, a urologist in Montpelier. I called and recounted my health history in detail with him over the phone, including the many pneumonias. I was at his office within a couple of days. Dr. Poplowski said, "We need some x-rays to see what may be the problem."

When I arrived at the x-ray department of the hospital on a snowy December morning, a smiling Dr. Poplowski was also there. "I'll get a look right away and we can discuss further treatment, if any," he said. I felt that I was in good hands.

After x-rays were completed I joined the radiologist and Dr. Poplowski. "Good news. We know the cause of your illnesses," the doctor said. He walked with me to a wall where the x-rays were posted. "See here?" pointing to some dark shadows. "This is your left kidney. See the shadow just above?" I nodded. "That dark spot is an undeveloped third kidney. And that is what made you sick. Urine backed up into this third kidney, stayed there and infected it and the left kidney also. That's when you got those back pains and high fevers." Made sense to me.

"But why did doctors think I had pneumonia?" I asked.
"The infected kidney sensitized surrounding areas, including the lower lobe of the left lung, and that's what doctors detected when you were examined," he explained.

I was stunned. "What do I do now, more medication?"

"No," he said. "We need to remove the left kidney. After years and years of infections, it is diseased. We need to schedule surgery for you. I probably can save a part and don't have to take the entire kidney. If your right kidney is not affected yet, you'll be fine. We only need one kidney."

My mind went blank. I couldn't think of any questions to ask and was very quiet. "Are you all right?" the doctor asked.

"Yes," I said, "I hadn't expected this. I need a little time to digest your news."

Dr. Poplowski continued, "Your right kidney probably has been doing all the work for years already. If it is healthy, you'll be all right."

The doctor explained that the procedure included removing one rib. "I'll also have to repair possible damage to the bladder and will schedule that surgery a couple of days after the kidney." He continued, "But, before I can operate we have to clear up this infection. That'll probably take three to six weeks." He looked at his calendar, "How is February 1st?"

"Fine," I nodded.

He continued, "The stronger antibiotic I'm prescribing will give you a yeast infection. Don't be concerned. I can prescribe something for that. Just give me a call. Be sure not to catch any colds or flu. If you're sick I cannot operate and will have to reschedule."

After Dr. Poplowski left, the radiologist said, "Why don't you sit down for a minute." He looked at me, "You're very lucky. Usually patients with your condition and at your age come to us in a coma. Often they cannot be saved." We chatted for a while. Then he said, "If I were you, I'd ask the doctor to remove the kidney completely. If they leave a partial kidney, you'll be back here in a few years for another surgery to remove that part." I appreciated that he was taking the time to give me clarifying background information.

I sat in my car for a while before driving home. I still couldn't quite grasp what was going to happen. I didn't know of anyone with only one kidney. I've only heard of people on dialysis. Will that be what I'll have to do if the other kidney is affected also? Many thoughts flashed through my mind: "Why?" "Why now?"

"How do I tell Trent and the children? I don't want anybody to worry. It's not fair!"

I drove away slowly thinking, "How come doctors didn't discover this in all these years? I bet my appendix wasn't the problem either when it was removed."

I was thinking of all the summer vacations that I spent in bed recuperating from 'pneumonia'! I realized that my urine always was cloudy. I didn't know that it was supposed to be clear, almost colorless. I gave countless urine samples during three pregnancies - not one doctor noticed!?

When I arrived home I had stopped wallowing. "It is what it is," I decided. Like the doctor said, I was lucky. I focused on that. Now that I knew I had a diseased kidney I found that thought repulsive. I wanted it out of my body and rid of it as soon as possible. February was two month away and it seemed like a long time to me. I wanted the kidney out now!

Staying healthy until surgery had to be my main focus now. I started working on a plan. I looked at surgery as a race date. Running had taught me to train for a race to have ultimate energy. That's what I wanted going into surgery.

To hopefully avoid a yeast infection and more medication, I increased my daily intake of yoghurt containing several varieties of probiotics to counteract the stronger antibiotics I had to take until surgery.

On the calendar, I worked out a training schedule. I would taper off the week before surgery with no running at all for three days. On February 1st, my body would be rested and full of energy. I visualized a speedy healing process.

When Trent came home I could calmly relay Dr. Poplowski's findings. Jason was at West Point, only Andrea and Derek were at home, and together with Trent they would manage while I was hospitalized for approximately two weeks. Andrea and Derek were fine with the thought that one kidney is all I needed to live a normal life.

I managed not to catch a cold; I also did not get a yeast infection. At the pre-surgery appointment Dr. Poplowski explained, "A third kidney is hereditary. It skips a generation and usually is found in females. You want to keep that in mind for your grandchildren"

"I didn't know that." Then I told him, "I have given this a lot of thought. I really would like you to remove the entire kidney."

Trent had to work the day before surgery; I drove myself to the hospital in the afternoon to check in. Surgery was scheduled for 8 a.m.; Trent would be there when I woke up.

From my appendix surgery when I was eleven, I clearly remembered the ether mask coming down on my face and it felt like I was suffocating. I had a nightmare of circling and circling above the ocean with large wings attached, desperately looking for a safe place to land. Years later, when hang-gliding became popular, I was reminded of my nightmare. It's one sport I made sure not to try.

The anesthesiologist assured me that I wouldn't know when I was going under. He was right, of course. He was talking to me one minute and next I heard Dr. Poplowski, "I removed the entire kidney. Your right kidney is very healthy." I was completely content.

In the recovery room Trent told me, "Dr. Poplowski walked into the waiting room after almost eight hours. I was getting very worried that something went wrong. Because before he went into the operating room he told me that it would take about five hours. His entire front was covered with blood, but he was smiling and said, "Resounding success. She'll be fine. I did the bladder surgery at the same time. Her strong constitution could take it."

Trent continued, "I'm glad this is over! I didn't want to lose you. I couldn't think about anything else." I could only nod.

After a day my head was no longer foggy from the anesthesia. I had two scars to heal. A vertical one on the left side of my rib cage and a horizontal one just above the bladder. Drainage tubes were attached to both. If I'm healing as expected, they could be removed within ten days. They only hurt if I coughed and that luckily didn't happen often. I took pain medication only when I absolutely needed it.

I started walking as soon as the nurse helped me to get out of bed; I wanted to be well and strong to be with Jason for parent's weekend at West Point in the middle of March. It was the first time parents were invited on campus during the freshman year.

Parent's Weekend

I was surprised how weak my body felt as I shuffled along the hallway. My runner's legs had turned to Jell-O. I was glad to have the rolling stand, draped with the various drainage tubes from my body, to hold on to.

Every day I pushed myself a bit farther, my legs were getting stronger and the shuffle changed to walking. Soon I walked twice a day, making long rounds on the entire hospital floor.

Not many patients were walking. The doors to all rooms were open. As I passed one after another I saw that most patients were either in bed or sitting in a chair by the bed. All rooms were filled. A few were like mine, a double room but with only one occupant. I was glad I didn't have a roommate. Nights were noisy. Nurses and other staff were constantly moving around and some patients were quite verbal throughout the night. I know I slept better without another sick person in the next bed.

After a week, while making his daily visit to check on my oxygen uptake, a therapist said, "I'm impressed, you're doing great for your age. I have never seen anyone your age recover from such a long operation so quickly." I knew my recovery was on track.

I heard "your age" often during encounters with doctors and nurses. I was 42, but they made it sound like I was at least 80! Every day, when I fell into my bed after walking, I had nothing to do but time to think. I felt that this surgery was a wake-up call and actually a blessing. The surgery could have turned out differently. It made me realize how vulnerable I was.

Life had been moving along at a busy pace. It was up to me to make changes. "Do I want to keep going like that?" "No," I decided. I don't want to be tied to my designer bag business for the next ten or twenty years. I've done all I could; built it from zero into a successful business. I had learned a lot about myself, but there must be other things I can do. "There are many years ahead. As soon as I've recovered, I will sell it," I promised myself.

"What will I do instead?" I had no idea. I was so focused on my business that nothing came to mind. I figured that by the time Heidi of Vermont* was sold, I would know.

◆◆◆

New Citizen

"Most of us in this room have never had to face a decision like this. We all take our citizenship, all its rights, privileges and duties, for granted."

With this opening statement, Chief Judge Albert W. Coffrin was about to begin the swearing in of the newest citizens of the United States of America. It was 1985 and I was about to become a naturalized American.

When I arrived in the United States in 1963, becoming a citizen never entered my mind. I had a green card, was working, traveling and observing the culture of this country. In Vermont, I married Trent and stayed. I missed my mother and greater family in Berlin. Aside from that, I settled happily into everyday life here.

Communicating was different from today. My mother didn't have a telephone until well into the 1970s. I wrote her every week about life here and she responded, usually by snail mail, with news about family and the old neighborhood.

After five years I was eligible to apply for U.S. citizenship. Becoming a citizen seemed the logical step to take. Trent and I had two children, just bought a house and I was here to stay. The Immigration and Naturalization office mailed the necessary papers. Filling out the forms was easy until I came to the oath I needed to sign:

> I hereby declare, on oath, that I absolutely and
> entirely renounce and abjure all allegiance and
> fidelity to any foreign prince, potentate, state or

> sovereignty, of whom or which I heretofore have
> been a subject or citizen;

When I read 'renounce and abjure,' I stopped. No way. I couldn't swear to that! All my family was still living in Germany.

> The oath continued:
> ....that I will support and defend the Constitution
> and laws of the United States of America against all
> enemies, foreign and domestic; that I will bear true
> faith and allegiance to the same; that I will bear
> arms on behalf of the United States when required
> by the law; that I will perform noncombatant
> service in the armed forces of the United States
> when required by the law; that I will perform work
> of national importance under civilian direction
> when required by the law; and I take this obligation
> freely without any mental reservation or purpose of
> evasion; so help me God.

The remainder of the oath made sense, but I had plenty of mental reservations. I could not take such an oath and was disappointed. Citizenship was not to be. By not becoming a citizen the only thing I wouldn't be able to do is vote.

"Well," I thought, "it'll just have to do. I'll try very hard to make my contribution to society, but voting will have to be done by the rest of the population. They can elect a new president without me."

Over the years I realized that being a responsible citizen involves more than voting in a presidential election every four years. It wasn't only presidential elections where I had to abstain. I could not vote – period.

I could not participate in any public event requiring a vote, right down to the local level. School issues, affecting my children, such as the budget, are decided every year and I could not vote. Every March, on Town Meeting Day in Vermont, residents decide where to spend the tax dollars and I could not cast my vote. Sure, I could have my opinions and go out and lobby. But when it came down to standing up and being counted, I had to pass. It's like preparing dinner and not being allowed to eat.

When Richard Nixon was president, I applied for citizenship again in 1972. I wanted to vote against him at the upcoming election. However, I still stumbled over the oath and left it at that.

It was not important to Trent, the children or my German family. The important part for my mother was that I had a family and a good life in America. Trent, the children and I didn't discuss citizenship for me. The children didn't even know that I was not a citizen. It really only mattered to me.

In the early spring of 1984, I spent two weeks in the hospital. I had lots of time to think and contemplate the future. More than twenty years had passed since I stepped onto American soil. Time left its mark. The eldest of our children was a freshman at West Point, the others were in junior high and high school. My life and interests were unquestionably in the United States now. I knew for certain I was not moving back to Germany.

'Renounce and abjure' no longer were the insurmountable hurdles. In order to carry out my civic duties fully, I should be voting. Most of the time I wasn't sure about issues in Germany any more. I had not voted there for years. I made up my mind. I decided that I could become a citizen and be proud of my heritage too. I applied for citizenship again. This time I completed the papers all the way, signed the oath and mailed them.

Along with the application came a U.S. history booklet with the suggestion that I study it closely. Trent and I would be called for an interview for final consideration. We should expect to answer questions together and I should be prepared to be quizzed. I was nervous. I studied and memorized all previous presidents and the constitution. Trent threw pop-quizzes my way often. "Who was the 5th President?"

"Oh...Ah...James Monroe, 1817 – two terms."

"Right!"

The appointment with the immigration officials was a cinch. I was called into the office first. The clerk checked my German passport, green card and Vermont driver's license. He handed all back and with a wink and declared, "I believe you are who you claim to be on the application."

Trent was asked to come in to join me. The official looked at our marriage certificate and property tax receipt that showed both our names and returned them to us. That was it. No pop quiz. I passed their criteria.

Finally the important day arrived. On May 1, 1985, Trent drove me to the courthouse in Burlington, Vermont. About 30 people were gathered in a small court room waiting to take the oath to become American citizens.

Color bearers from a VFW Post in Burlington carried the flags of the United States and state of Vermont to the front of the room. A clerk asked us, one by one, to stand.

Judge Coffrin stepped up, looked at us and said, "Repeat after me." He recited the Pledge of Allegiance to the United States, a few words at a time. I was relieved that he was wise enough to do that. My mind was blank, I couldn't think of the words. I listened and took my oath. Tears welled up but were quickly forgotten when everyone cheered after, "liberty and justice for all."

Come election time, for whatever or whomever, I am there. Whether my cause wins or loses is not that important. To me, voting is.

◆◆◆

Crew Chief

———•———•———

While honeymooning in St. Jovite, Canada, we were walking through the lobby of the Grey Rocks Inn. Suddenly Trent let go of my hand and rushed out the front door. "It's Bruce McLaren's car!" Parked in the driveway was a trailer, carrying the shiny orange CanAm car of the New Zealand racing great.

We were thrilled! I found out that Trent is a car racing fan from way back, like me. We had no idea that our honeymoon destination had brought us so close to the fairly new St. Jovite race track in Quebec.

Trent is from upstate New York and spent many Sundays at the Watkins Glen track with his father. Those were the days when fans could walk into the pits, get close to the cars, and talk to the drivers. It became Trent's secret ambition to drive a race car someday.

While growing up in Germany, I always wanted to go to car races. Events were held regularly at the nearby Avus Ring at the edge of Berlin. Sometimes I could see cars maneuvering a high banked corner when the city train I was riding rumbled by the track. I wanted to watch a race so badly! No one I knew was remotely interested. It was unthinkable that I could go by myself.

The closest I came to going to a track was when I visited my Uncle Adrian in West Germany. He also was a fan and didn't miss many races at the nearby Nurburgring. I was there for a few days and Uncle Adrian took me to the race track. It was mid-week and the place was deserted. The only car noise was the humming of his tired Opel. We were sitting in his car while he told me some racing stories about this world famous track. At that moment it was the most exciting place in the world to me.

On this Wednesday morning in June of 1965, after admiring the McLaren car from all possible angles, we set out to find the race track. It wasn't difficult to locate. But we were too early. The track was locked up tight. We could only peek through the fence. St. Jovite would be open the next day, but we would be on our way back to Vermont by then.

Shortly after our return home, Trent bought a bright yellow Bultaco racing bike. Trent and a bunch of similarly outfitted friends started racing each other in empty fields. Then they discovered organized motorcycle racing, a very new sport in the U.S. Trent began competing in the amateur division all over New England. The children and I spent many Sundays trackside watching. Other racers' families comprised many of the spectators. The children always had plenty of playmates. Along with a picnic between races, those outings were fun.

The boys always knew where Dad was – in the garage. Together they tuned the bike to perfection over and over. With job demands, the commitment to racing became increasingly difficult with not enough time for practice sessions. After seven years of active competition, Trent retired from bike racing.

At about the same time Paul Newman, already in his 40s, started racing cars. Appropriately, the theory that you had to be a young hotshot to get started in racing went out the window. Trent was still hoping, maybe someday?

Someday arrived in the mid 1980s. I gave Trent his dream birthday present, a three-day Road Racing School package with Bertil Roos, a former Formula 1 driver, in the Poconos in Pennsylvania. Trent was surprised and delighted and started to plan for the school in early October.

What I didn't know was that Trent also was looking into buying a used racing car. He dropped a few hints here and there like, "After driving school I really would like to go racing!" The real estate consulting business was very successful. He figured that he could afford it now.

A month after his birthday Trent pulled into our driveway with a Ferrari red Crossle open wheel racer on a trailer. He got out of the car beaming, "All along I was looking in the rearview mirror checking to see if the car was real!"

Trent signed up for driving sessions at Lime Rock Park in Connecticut to qualify for a national racing license.

Lime Rock, as it is referred to, had hosted many national races and was revered by all race drivers. It features a notorious downhill section, known as one of the scariest stretches of race track in America.

Trent converted part of our sheep barn into a garage. There he worked on the car, and learned how it needed to be maintained. He also spray-painted the body a metallic midnight blue. We christened the car "Blue Bullet. "The Sports Car Club of America – SCCA - granted his request of the number 33 for his car. White 33s were carefully applied to the hood and both sides of the car.

I put my head into the garage a few times. I was going to be the crew and got pointers about the fuel cell, starter motor and where to find the dipstick for checking the oil. I was looking forward to going to race tracks with Trent.

On a few weekends we went to a small track in New Hampshire. This venue is now the Loudon track, hosting NASCAR and Indy Car races. Trent was testing himself and the car in small amateur club sessions. Drivers took laps around the track in staggered starts. There was no passing, and cars were timed individually.

Every outing was also a test for me. I had to check and re-check nuts and bolts, test the seat belts, gauge tire pressure and take tire temperatures. It was especially crucial to have the tire pressure correct. Sometimes Trent came off the track saying, "Better check the tires. The car is handling a bit off." Sure enough, the tire pressure was low when I tested it.

While Trent was on the track, I timed laps and learned how and where to give signals if needed. Often I was changing tires after a session. The Crossle didn't have gas or oil gauges and I checked their levels constantly. I also made sure none of the nuts and bolts got loose, tested the starting battery to be sure it was fully charged and polished the car when the to-do list was completed.

We found that fellow racers were a helpful community, ready to loan spare parts or a splash of fuel. Trent earned his racing license in the fall after the Bertil Roos School.

The first official SCCA race was the following April at Lime Rock. We both believed that we were ready.

It rained heavily the night before the race. On race day, it poured, it drizzled, it stopped, and so it went. I changed from rain tires to regular treads several times. Spare tires were fully mounted on a set of wheel rims.

After Trent was already lined up on the track, it started pouring again and the countdown to the race halted. Tools and rain tires where already trackside, just in case. Everyone changed tires right on the track. We had to be quick. I was nervous, as it was my first tire change under pressure. I didn't want to miss a step in the sequence: Jack up the car; all tires off and wheeled to the side; rain tires on. I wanted to be sure to tighten the wheels' lug nuts just right. As a rule the nuts were only slightly tightened at first. After the car was lowered, the wheels were securely fastened and tire pressure was re-checked.

Crew chief at work

"Qualifying for a starting position is the most nerve-wracking," Trent said. Every minute steering change could affect your lap time. Where and how hard you braked going into corners also could make a huge difference. Drivers turned three laps on the track. The best time of those was used to line up the field for the race. I made mental notes as I watched the different approaches drivers took. Trent qualified to start in the middle of the 38 car field.

Finally the race was on. Many engines created a constant racket as cars maneuvered the track: a deep roar as they raced up a hill; a split second pause when changing gears; a high-pitched whine when they accelerated across the start/finish line on the long straightaway. I knew where cars were by their sounds. It was a symphony unlike any other.

From my vantage point I could see several stretches of the track. Flashes of colors sped by in the distance. I could easily spot Trent's blue Crossle. I timed each lap as he crossed the starting line and quickly marked it on the clipboard. After 15 laps around the 2.5 mile track, he finished without spinning out. He accomplished his goal of not coming in last. He was fifth in the open wheel class!

I got all lap times correctly. Finally I was involved and useful at a race track. I loved it! We went to many race courses, but never made it back to St. Jovite.

Now I knew the race car inside and out, but driving one was still on my wish list. One bold day I signed up for a One Day Racing School session at the Skip Barber Driving School at Lime Rock.

Trent came with me, and this time he was standing by the track watching. Just like his first race, the skies opened and it poured all day.

School started at 8 a.m. There were five students, and I was the lone woman. We introduced each other nervously with a nod to the sky, "What a morning!"

First came a classroom session. The instructor highlighted the best route around the track, "Start breaking before you get to a turn. Then step on the gas and you'll be able to go faster around the corner." Sounded simple enough to me.

Then we went outside and were introduced to our car parked on pit lane. I climbed into the cockpit and felt lost. I couldn't see above the steering wheel nor could I reach the pedals! Although the school had asked for height and weight when I registered, they didn't set up the car for my 5'1" frame. Now they jacked up the seat and scrambled to add several layers of padding until I could actually see the track. They extended and padded the pedals so that I could drive the car.

All along it was raining hard. Even though I was wearing raingear, I was soaked and shivering within a few minutes after sitting in the open cockpit.

Finally we were cleared to go. "We're sending you out for a test lap. Just follow each other and come back to this spot." I started the engine and then we were off. Slowly. I could hardly see the brake light of the car in front of me. Low clouds and a huge rooster tail spray created a visibility problem. My car barely reached 50 mile per hour before we drove back into the pit lane.

One young man scrambled out of the cockpit. "I quit! These conditions are horrible." I couldn't agree more. But unless the school canceled the session, I was determined to keep driving.

Back on the track I practiced braking before the apex, the starting point of a corner. The car started to wiggle if I was going too fast for the conditions. Trent's advice flashed through my mind, "A wet track makes both breaking and speeding up more challenging."

"Better be cautious," I decided. I slowed down, and then I slowed down some more. The speedometer never reached 100 mph on a track where you could safely drive 180. I didn't dare go any faster around the wide sweeping curves or the tight essess (several turns in a row). On the downhill it felt like I was losing traction and curbed the speed again. Every lap was white-knuckle driving.

Finally the instructor signaled "last lap." I felt relieved. I could stop with my pride intact. I wasn't "the woman who quit." Parked again on pit road, I could hardly pry my fingers off the steering wheel. I wiggled out of the cockpit and relaxed for the first time that day.

I would have loved to be driving on the track on a sunny day. Regardless, I am really happy to have had my laps around Lime Rock and a little taste of racing.

◆◆◆

Patient Heal Thyself

"Trent it looks like you have Candida, a yeast infection." Dr. Wade said after reviewing Trent's long list of ailments.

"How come? I thought this is a woman's disease." Trent asked.

"Well, you have yeast gone rampant throughout your body, including the brain. I'm battling it myself." Dr. Wade continued, "There is no specific treatment. The best you can do is read about it and help yourself." He reached behind his desk and showed Trent a copy of *The Yeast Connection.* "It is the only source with in-depth information. I find it very helpful." Then he said, "For starters we need to restore your intestinal flora."

Is Dr. Wade going to lead us out of the fog? We were both buoyed by that possibility. It had been a long journey, stretching five years, without any helpful news.

It started in the fall of 1984. Trent came home early from his daily training run. "I can't run. Every time I land on my left foot a sharp pain shoots up. It's impossible." We had been running and competing in road races for years.

He consulted doctors at a racing clinic. "You'll need inserts to support your arch. You'll be running again soon." Inserts didn't help. Trent stopped running.

Trent was a partner in a real estate consulting company in Burlington. He made the 120-mile round-trip to his office Monday through Friday. He also was varsity ice hockey coach at our local high school during the winter.

At roughly the same time when Trent stopped running, he started to come home early from the office in the middle of the week. Completely exhausted and with what felt like the flu, he went straight to bed. With the telephone close by, he worked from his bed the remainder of the week. He did rally and got up for evening hockey practices or weekend games. After resting he usually felt better and was ready to go back to his office. He thought he had beaten the flu.

But flu and fatigue came back. Trent came home even earlier and headed to bed with barely enough energy for a good-night hug. A doctor's appointment, to ascertain if he had a lingering case of the flu, didn't help. "No, your system seems to be ok. You're probably working too much."

Jason and Andrea were off at college; Derek was the only one still at home. We just accepted that Trent couldn't beat his sore throat and annoying ailments like joint and muscle aches. Again we thought not running and extra rest surely would help.

"You know, I always feel worse after I've been at the hockey rink," he said one winter morning. He continued, "My mold allergy is probably acting up. I'll be better come spring."

Well, he wasn't. Exposure to mold was everywhere in the damp and cool northeastern climate. During several of his frequent road trips, I got disturbing phone calls from Trent. Once during a coaching clinic at a hockey arena, another time when staying at on older, moldy motel: "I'm fine. I'm calling from the emergency room. Don't worry, I'm fine. I passed out and was taken to the hospital by ambulance. Really, I'm fine."

After testing him carefully, doctors couldn't determine that anything was out of order. "You're probably stressed out. A little rest and you'll be fine." I was restless whenever Trent was away, hoping all would be well.

Eventually his fatigue had become extreme. He now went to the office only on Mondays. Often I was driving him, because even that was exhausting. Luckily his partner Chip took over Trent's responsibilities without one complaint.

Our routines revolved around monitoring Trent's condition. With Trent's fatigue accelerating, our activities and social life came to a stand-still. We often had dinner parties but that also became a challenge. Sometimes it was already afternoon before I knew if Trent could rally, when he said, "I'm ok, I'll get up in a little while." A couple of times he felt really exhausted, but it was too late to call off our invitation. I would be the one totally wasted after those dinners, worrying the entire time if Trent would make it through the evening. We stopped planning dinners and declined invites as well.

We were puzzled that doctors could not determine what the source of Trent's condition might be. From Massachusetts to California, he consulted clinics in hopes of finding answers. The results were always the same. "All tests are negative. Stress is probably the main reason. You're doing too much. Vacations, for a change of pace, will do you good."

Trent came home from these consultations totally dejected, which was not his usual state of mind. He would be really depressed for days - only rallying when he had to.

We were both helpless. It seemed like we were engulfed by a dense, heavy fog and couldn't find a way out. Would we have to live like this forever? We were in our forties with many years yet to live. I didn't dare think ahead, just dealing with the day at hand. I did all I could to be supportive. Trent was the one with the challenge and he didn't complain – never felt sorry for himself, but everything affected me as well. I felt I needed an outlet to maintain my sanity.

I started going to movies by myself when Trent wasn't up to it. That was probably the biggest step. "You go ahead," he'd say, "it'll do you good." We both knew that I was his sole support and needed some outside stimulants to be able to continue. From road running to farming and car racing, we had done everything together. I joined a writing group and regularly went to a German club meetings in Burlington. Sometimes I had a twinge of guilt when I drove off and Trent was sleeping. But it also felt good to get away.

Other joint activities also ceased. The Sunday ritual of reading the New York Times together turned into a solo activity. Newsprint made Trent sick immediately. So I read the paper and relayed or read interesting items to him. Exposure to gas fumes at race tracks made Trent unable to get out of bed for days. He stopped car racing – a lifelong ambition that he accomplished a few years before.

Trent finally resigned as varsity coach, citing ill health. Since he didn't know what he was dealing with, he couldn't be specific. A couple of weeks later a friend and mother of a hockey player said to Derek, "Well, is your dad enjoying a miraculous recovery?"

Derek asked me, "What does she mean?"

"She implied that Trent was making up an illness as an excuse to quit coaching."

I was stunned and insulted. After 19 years of coaching in the community, she thought he made up being sick? Knowing how he had struggled to honor that obligation, I felt like throwing something. I avoided running into her, not trusting myself as to what I might say.

We followed up on even the remotest possibility of getting to the bottom of his ills. Even AIDS seemed like a likely culprit. Many sufferers exhibited symptoms like Trent's. Could he be infected? How? I had lengthy surgery in 1984. Did I get a transfusion of tainted blood that infected Trent? I called my doctor. He told me, "I checked your records. No. You didn't need any blood." We kept searching.

Bills for hospitalizations, ambulances, a multitude of tests and doctor fees were piling up. Trent's company carried the best health insurance program available. The insurance company didn't cover any of our costs because claims were not based on an official disease. We refinanced our house a couple of times. Our resources were shrinking.

After five years of getting his hopes dashed again and again Trent said to me, "The only place I have not consulted is the Mayo Clinic. I'll call Dr. Wade to set a referral. I'm not leaving there until I have answers."

That's when Trent's health slowly improved. He bought the book Dr. Wade recommended right away. He read how diet affects yeast and stopped his beloved sweets. Sugar feeds yeast. Alcohol also feeds yeast, "No more wine or beer," he decided.

He checked in regularly with Dr. Wade. After six weeks he said, "Trent, you should be better by now. There may be something else." Fog was closing in again. Trent had to continue his quest for help.

Trent found Dr. Warnock, a naturopathic physician in Burlington. After extensive testing he concluded that Trent had Chronic Fatigue Syndrome, referred to as CFS. He explained, "Your immune system is nonexistent, and your body has no defenses whatsoever. Very little is known about CFS. It has multiple triggers, among them: nutritional deficiency, stress and immune dysfunction. The illness resembles Lyme disease, mononucleosis, MS, Lupus, Candida, and others. Patients often have one of those, along with CFS; Candida in your case, Trent."

In the 1980s, CFS was an unknown illness; some doctors actually prescribed antibiotics, making things worse.

Trent had weekly treatments of antibiotics for four years for childhood allergies. "That damaged your immune system," Dr. Warnock pointed out. He continued, "Years of unknowingly feeding yeast with sugar and alcohol intake made yeast go out of control. Rampant yeast killed good bacteria in your digestive tract. One of the ripple effects is actually malnutrition. It takes many years before symptoms appear."

Dr. Warnock prescribed holistic supplements to strengthen Trent's immune system.

It all made sense. We were hoping that this time Trent may have a chance of recovery. Would this be the way to a healthier and normal life for both of us?

Trent designed an even stricter diet for himself. His meals now were void of anything that would feed his yeast: sugar, flours, fermented foods, fruits and beer and wine. Foods containing antibiotics like meat, farm-raised fish and all dairy also were off limits. He was fasting regularly to help cleanse his body.

At first I cooked two dinners nightly; one for Trent and one for myself. He ate mostly vegetables and rice. Sometimes I combined foods. This became a source of contention. On mornings when he wasn't well, he'd ask, "What was in the sauce or in the meat loaf?" When he concluded the food to be the source of the malaise that day, I felt incredibly guilty.

Sometimes he'd say, "Really, are you sure you didn't add anything else?" After quite a few of these incidents I said, "Why don't you cook some of the meals yourself. Then you'll know exactly what you're eating. I'm trying everything I know how to and it doesn't seem to be right."

Trent cooked some dinners, strictly adhering to the recipe according to his needs. He found that he still had bad mornings. I was elected to cook again.

Trent was a model patient. Slowly he was sick less often and his energy improved. "It's easy to follow a strict regiment when I can see the results," he said.

It was harder for me to notice. Trent's weight dropped from 165 to 123 pounds. This drastic loss made his 6' 2" frame look like a skeleton. He looked like a big puff of wind could carry him away. There was little left of my athletic husband.

Trent's condition kept improving. He could even savor the occasional glass of red wine without setbacks. Finally the dense fog had lifted and we were in charge of our lives again.

Dr. Warnock had other patients suffering like Trent. He felt that his success would give them hope and was referring some to Trent. Feeling that he had contained this demon, he was eager to help others. He learned that not everyone, even people worse off than he was, could follow a strict diet.

One woman, who was working at IBM, had been sent to a psychiatrist many times after the onset of her fatigue. Disability was denied and she couldn't find relief anywhere. Her reaction to Trent's suggestion was, "Give up sweets? I can't do that!"

After several calls from sufferers and long conversations, Trent started to keep the talks short when he realized people were looking for a simple solution. There just wasn't one.

By 1992, he considered himself 80% recovered; he was able to work full- time again.

There was the niggling mold allergy, however. Trent was no longer spending time at moldy hockey arenas, but mold was everywhere. We decided that a change in climate might help and be the last piece of the puzzle to recovery. Trent accepted a sales position on Bald Head Island, off the coast of North Carolina.

We had to leave our home of almost 30 years, the only one our children had known. "This is harder to take than any of my misery," Trent kept saying.

I knew that we didn't have a choice. We sold our heavily mortgaged house, salvaging a little cash for starting over.

Trent has maintained a careful diet and periodic cleanses. Except for rare flare-ups, he has been well.

◆◆◆

P.S.: In 2008, more than twenty years after the onset of his symptoms, the Center for Disease Control officially recognized CFS as an illness. There is still neither medication nor a cure for Chronic Fatigue Syndrome.

Cook-Off Adventure

Calling all cooks! The National Beef Industry Council was inviting entries using economy cuts of beef for their annual cook-off, their largest promotion, in 1986. I had been using economy cuts for years and thought, "Why not? I'll send my ragout recipe." I typed a clean copy of the recipe, suggested it be served on a bed of noodles and mailed it.

Since I sold my business I had a more flexible schedule. Jason and Andrea were off at college. Derek, a high school sophomore, and Trent could easily fend for themselves now and then when I went on one of my cook-off adventures. I had been to several contests ranging from bread, to soup, to chicken. I always was looking forward to meeting other foodies.

In June, I received a call from the cook-off's headquarters. "You are the winner from Vermont with Beef Ragout Country Style." I hadn't given the cook-off much thought and was totally surprised.

"We are inviting you to the cook-off in Michigan in September. You'll get all the details by mail, but we wanted you to know." This was the most prestigious cook-off yet in which I would be competing. I couldn't wait to tell the family. "Good for you! My favorite - Why don't you cook it tonight?" Trent said.

Complete instructions soon followed. The cook-off was going to be at the Hyatt Regency in Dearborn, Michigan, where everyone also would be staying. The council would set up individual cooking stations with electric stoves. It also would supply the beef. It was my responsibility to bring whatever I needed to prepare my dish according to the recipe, including pots and pans and garnish for presentation.

I left nothing to chance. The first to go into my carry-on bag was the orange cast iron Le Creuset pot for the ragout, all wrapped in protective towels. I added a smaller one to cook the noodles, followed by a cutting board, knives, spoons, a heavy-duty pepper grinder and any utensils that I might possibly need. Garlic, onions, olives, mushrooms and red wine in a jar were packed just before leaving on a Sunday.

The heavy bags made a racket as I boarded the plane and brought curious looks from fellow passengers. "I'm going to a cooking contest and have to bring my pots," was the opener to fun conversation and lots of, "We'll be rooting for you. Best of luck."

The Beef Council treated us like VIPs for three days. It started with a red carpet welcome at the airport. Mary Hagar, my personal assistant provided by the beef council, drove me to the hotel. Mary was a member of the American National Cattlewomen and volunteered at the cook-off every year. She ushered me to the reception desk, where I was handed the room key just by saying my name.

That same evening the Beef Council hosted a welcome reception for the contestants, four men and forty-four women, and their assistants. Everyone was excited and the room was humming with constant chatter.

At 6:30 Monday morning, two buses took us to a supermarket that was open only to us. The idea was to select our preferred cuts of beef without hassle. As soon as we were inside, the store suddenly was dark. A glance to the outside confirmed that the power failure was not only in this store. "Stay wherever you are. The clerks are getting flashlights," a voice in the dark reassured us. Soon, the clerks led our group to the meat counter.

My needs were simple. The ragout recipe called for a two-pound boneless piece of chuck roast. The butcher handed the wrapped beef to me within a minute. This shopping-in-the-dark adventure became fodder for endless jokes and set a light tone throughout the day.

The next stop was the convention center where the competition would take place. Several rows of cooking stations – 24 in all, each with a stove, prepping table and a jumbo roll of paper towels, filled the cavernous convention room. One door led to a smaller hall where the judges would taste the recipes from 9 a.m. to 4 p.m. I inspected the small kitchen set-up and unpacked my tools to be ready for Tuesday – contest day.

While I was reviewing all steps from start to finish, I realized that I didn't bring a platter for presentation. I mistakenly thought we would serve our recipe on plates for the judges. No. The entire meal needed to be presented on a platter as was mentioned in the recipe I submitted. Now what do I do? Where could I scrounge up a serving platter? Maybe at the hotel? Mary saved me. "There's a large mall, including Macy's, attached to the convention center. You can surely find something there after lunch."

Mary was a jewel to have in my corner. She was calm and competent. It probably served her well at the cattle business she and her husband had in Iowa. I couldn't wait for the formal luncheon to be over. I found an off-white pottery platter at Macy's; it would show off the ragout perfectly. Now I could relax.

Another bus trip took us to the Henry Ford Museum & Greenfield Village. Greenfield Village is a restored turn-of-the-century village complete with a general store. The adjacent museum featured everything old - from kitchen tools to automobiles, including the first Model-T. The beef council hosted a buffet reception for us with food stations throughout the museum. Our conversations were all about food.

On cook-off day I didn't have to rush. There was plenty of time before I needed to be at the judges' door at noon. I went to my station early anyway. As soon as I stepped out of the elevator, there was no doubt that the competition had begun. The aromas of sautéed onions and spices mingled beyond the hall. Some contestants were already cooking. The first dish had to be ready for the judges by 9a.m.

Mary was early also and greeted me with a cheery "Good morning, Heidi! Ready?"

I wasn't nervous; my recipe was like an old friend. I had made it at least a hundred times. If I needed something, Mary was there. She hovered within shouting distance. I started cutting the chunk of beef into cubes, chopped the onions and mushrooms and set all aside until it was time to heat my pot. It was eerily quiet in this large room. Chopping sounds and clanging of lids onto pots was what I heard - very little conversation. Once the ragout was simmering, Mary guarded my station and I could visit with the other contestants.

The room was open to the public. Along with a light crowd of onlookers, I was making my way from one cook to the other. I was curious and wanted to see what my competition was prepping. The smell of hot oil, curries and garlic filled the large room. Except for the posted recipes, it was hard to get an actual sense of what the finished dishes were like. Recipes ranged from Korean, Japanese, Greek and Mexican specialties to roasts and many variations of beef salad. A man from Delaware was making "Beef Ragout," a dish similar to mine.

I kept checking and tasting the ragout. It was ready with 15 minutes to spare. All turned out perfectly, especially the beef, I thought. It was tender and moist. I kept the platter warm to put the noodles and ragout on it at the last minute.

A television crew stopped by. While the camera was rolling, they asked, "Where did you learn the recipe?"

"It's a combination of German and French recipes."

Ready for the judges

Official photos of the dish were taken before I marched my platter to the judges' chamber with applause by the other contestants. Mary said, "I'll clean up before the next competitor comes. Don't worry about a thing."

"Oh, thank you. I tried not to make too much of a mess."

It was noon and a long time until the awards banquet. I went back to the mall for some leisurely window shopping.

We were asked to pose for a group photo at 5p.m. Then we lined up outside the dining room by state to be announced as we were entering one at a time. During previous lunches and dinners, we mostly talked about families, cooking and traveling. Now the chatter turned to prizes. Suddenly people were nervous. One woman jabbered to no one in particular, "Oh, I hope I get something. This is my third time with the beef cook-off." I had no such qualms, but was looking forward to find out what the panel of seven judges deemed worthy.

While we were waiting, a brightly smiling Mary stopped by for a good-bye hug, as she had to catch her plane, "It was a pleasure working with you."

Then we were inching towards the main event. Once my name was announced, I stepped through the door illuminated by flood lights and found my seat at the elevated rows of tables facing the audience.

Naturally, roast beef was served. We were still eating when the prize winners, starting with Honorable Mentions, were announced. Every time a name was called we paused to applaud. Then came 5th, 4th, and 3rd place winners, I was not among the lucky. "2nd place for "Beef Ragout..." - a long pause followed. "Oh," I thought, "he won. Well, this was so much fun, I think I'll try again."

The announcer continued, "...Country Style is awarded to Vermont contestant Heidi Smith." I was stunned. My body was tingling all the way to my toes. I was speechless as I got hugged by my table neighbors. I had never won anything this large. The red cocktail dress I was wearing prompted the piano entertainer to sing "Lady in Red," a current hit from the movie Working Girl.

I floated to the stage. I'm sure I thanked the Beef Council and complemented them on such a well-organized event. I can't remember. I probably had dessert, but I can't remember.

I do remember the media event after dinner. The three top award winners were ushered into another reception room where we were interviewed by television crews and reporters from many newspapers. Finally we could go back to the main reception where we were greeted again by applause.

One of the judges, Toni Allegra, food editor with the San Diego Tribune, approached me. "Most dishes were easy to judge and categorize," she told me. "But we had a tie between first and second place and were in a stalemate for over an hour. I think you should know that your beef was cooked to perfection. The best of all entries. What eventually broke the tie was that Hot Hunan Hoagies – sliced top round steak served on a bun - was more fitting for today's trend towards fast dinner preparation."

That compliment actually meant the most to me. I was recognized for what I was striving for every time I cook.

When the crowd disbursed I called Trent. "Guess what?!! I got second place!"

"I knew you would do well!" I could hear the smile in his words while Derek and my mother, who was visiting, were cheering in the background.

A card from Mary was in my room. She had seen the list of winners before leaving. I don't know who was more excited. She wrote, "This was amazing! I have been a cook-off volunteer for many years. You are my first winner!"

Back in Vermont, the publicity became an unexpected boost for my catering business that I started in Burlington. Suddenly it went from fledgling enterprise to a busy, year-round venue.

◆◆◆

Beef Ragout Country Style
4 – 6 servings

2 pounds chuck roast, cut into 1 ¼-inch cubes
2 tablespoons oil
3 large onions cut into eight chunks
4 large garlic cloves, minced
1 teaspoon thyme
3 tablespoons Italian parsley, chopped
⅛ teaspoon salt and freshly ground pepper each
1 large can tomatoes, drained and tomatoes quartered
1 cup red wine – more if needed
½ cup beef broth
½ pound mushrooms, quartered
1 small can black olives
2 tablespoons parsley chopped

Heat the oil in a large Dutch oven and sear the meat. Do not crowd, do in batches if necessary,
Add onions, stir and brown lightly. Then push mixture to sides and add garlic to bottom of pot. Stir garlic for a minute to bring out flavor. Add tomatoes, thyme, salt, pepper and three tablespoons parsley and mix. Add wine and just enough broth to cover everything and bring to a boil. Cover, reduce heat and simmer for 1 hour.*
Add mushrooms and simmer another 30 minutes, or until beef is tender.
Adjust seasonings, add olives, remaining parsley and reheat.

*Can be cooked several days in advance to this point.

*Berlin 1989 - When the Wall Came Down**

"We have to change our thinking. Suddenly nothing is impossible anymore," an older man next to me reflected, as I was watching a sea of East Germans spill through the Wall into West Berlin, my hometown.

November 9, 1989 brought a new milestone in history. The Berlin Wall crumbled.

This was the first good news since the end of the war. I immediately bought a plane ticket from New York to Berlin, to celebrate with my family.

West Berlin was in an early Christmas-rush chaos. My reserved, elderly mother, light-footed like a teenager and bursting with excitement, tried to relay all events at once.

She told me how the Russian cellist Mstislav Rostropovich, moved deeply by the East Germans' action, chartered a private plane from his Paris residence and went directly to Checkpoint Charlie. Below the new Wall graffiti "Charlie retired," he played a half-hour of Bach in memory of those who died trying to escape.

"Can you believe it yet?" she continued. "They are free! It's monumental; it can make a sick person well."

* (Published by *The Times Argus,* Barre, Vermont)

I couldn't wait to go to the Wall. Mother and I went to one of the new crossings at Potsdamer Strasse near the Brandenburg Gate.

Heavy pedestrian traffic headed towards the Wall. We were swallowed by the crowd. I got butterflies, like waiting for my first date. Finally, a big gap in the Wall was in sight.

Jammed like sardines, we watched thousands of East Germans test the new policy. Going across the border with just a stamp in your passport? Unheard of! East German police, *Vopos*, actually smiled and merely waved people by.

As they crossed over, we cheered and applauded in the cold until hoarse. They waved back and slowly filed by, five or six across, like a slow motion movie. Exuberant shouts of, "*Willkommen!*...Isn't it great!...Where are you from?" filled the air.

Many would stop for a moment, take a deep breath, look around, and with a teary smile hug whoever was close. Suddenly I dissolved into tears of relief and joy. I was so proud of their courage. They are really free! Despite the evidence in front of me it was difficult to absorb the fundamental changes.

Men and women around us were wiping away tears, shaking their heads and murmuring, "I can't believe it...I can't believe it." People kept coming. After a while they all looked the same, turning into an undulating, endless ribbon of muted blue and gray.

Moving around the city was a challenge. Lines everywhere! Once in a bus or store, it was nearly impossible to get out. Getting to work was a major production for Berliners. "My ride usually takes fifteen minutes," an irritated cashier told me. "Today our bus couldn't get on the belt-way. Gridlock! It took an hour, and I had to stand all the way! But I'm sure it'll let up after the holidays," she added with a shrug.

The German Democratic Republic's (GDR) miniature cars, Trabants, have no emission control. Because their special gas mixture is not available in the West, they kept running out of gas and clogging the roads.

Berlin's administration slowly turned the city into a somewhat orderly madhouse. To ease traffic and pollution, the mayor of West Berlin, Walter Momper, appealed to East Germans to park their cars at the border and use the public transportation free of charge.

Greyhound buses from West Germany helped the taxed transportation department. Bus drivers, in unfamiliar territory, often got help from natives calling out bus stops.

Because the East's ancient phone system was out of order, *Vopos* and West Berlin traffic police installed army field telephones to coordinate additional crossings. Within a few days bulldozers and cranes tore thirteen new holes into the Wall. Now there are twenty-five crossings in an out of West Berlin. Traffic was heaviest at crossings close to West Berlin's center.

East Germans were showered with gifts at border crossings. Coca Cola, Mars Bars, soap, detergent samples, and more, were handed out. Kaiser's, a grocery store chain, gave away 170,000 bags containing a pound of coffee and a chocolate bar. Young women bundled up against the cold, welcomed men, women and children with carnations sent by Holland. Because West Berlin is blanked out on all road maps printed in the GDR, visitors received a city map.

The Morgenpost, Berlin's major daily, printed a special travel guide to ease the adjustment to a strange city. It featured: a subway and bus map, complete with time schedules; traffic laws and road signs; bank locations, shopping districts and information centers. All free or reduced fees for museums, concerts, theaters, and movies were listed. Practical tips – i.e., enter buses in front, exit to the rear, and "It pays to shop around" (East Germany has a uniform pricing system) – were also included.

By now, the normally stoic East Germans were moving about either happily smiling or totally dazed. They repaid the goodwill with politeness, cheerfulness and generally by coming out of their shell.

The Red Cross, Salvation Army, and the French, British and American armies pitched tents at all crossings and throughout the city. They assisted with information, hot food, and makeshift shelters in gyms. People had been sleeping in their cars, huddled in malls, hotel lobbies and subway stations.

Radio station SFB functioned as a clearinghouse for private homes offering a free room, sometimes just a living room sofa. After the first week, over 24,000 private accommodations became available.

The flow of humanity was unending. After ten days of the new policy, 12.3 of the total 16.7 million East Germans had travel visas. Border police counted over 800,000 people going into West Berlin in one day and finally gave up counting. But, as the authorities had hoped, only a fraction requested permanent stay in the West.

Buses and charter planes brought in thousands of tourists wanting to witness history. I must have given directions in English to at least half of them. Four lads from Ireland in Berlin for the day, wanted to know: "How far to the Wall? Where's the best crossing to watch people come over? Do we have to wait long to get into East Berlin? How do we get to the 'Spy Bridge'? What's the quickest route back to the airport?" They would be able to fit everything into the day, except the bridge.

Until November 9th, only selected diplomats were allowed to cross Glienicker Brücke, nicknamed Spy Bridge. It crosses the Havel River to Potsdam in a wooded, remote, rural section of Berlin. It's true, East and West exchanged spies here at odd hours through the mist rising from the river for years. Today it's one of the new crossings.

Laws regulating store and banking hours were suspended. Restaurants and shops remained open after hours and on Sundays. Extra help was hired. Some Berliners volunteered. One woman walked into a coffee house on the *Kurfürsten Damm*, "Do you need any help?" The owner grabbed her immediately. "Please! If you would make coffee. We can't keep up."

Bank clerks worked seven days a week to hand out 100 German marks ($55) welcome money, issued by the West German government. During the first three days, 135 million Marks were paid out in West Berlin.

East Germans are used to standing in line early at home if they want to get any of the sparse merchandise. Crowds milled patiently at the shops in West Berlin long before they opened. They were amazed at the supply in the West. Even when goods were sold out the previous day, shelves were stocked again the following morning.

People, three and four deep, marveled at window displays. Everything from hardware to food was thoroughly eyed and discussed. "Why so many kinds of salami?" one woman wondered. "You only need one!"

Families dominated the crowd. Baby carriages were loaded with packages like shopping carts. Everyone carried white plastic shopping bags bulging with sought after fruits and meats. It seemed that every family bought a boom box.

Toiletries, cosmetics, watches, toys, walk-mans, chocolates, and disposable diapers were hot sellers. And bananas. Bananas are unheard of in the GDR. Groups of three, four, and more, eating bananas huddled on sidewalks everywhere.

West Berliners in the street helped as soon as they saw anyone consulting a map, and I was happy to do my part. When heading in the same direction, I took people along and used the opportunity to ask their impressions and thoughts.

"We have to catch up with twenty-eight years of progress," one man said in awe. "After free elections, re-building can begin in earnest."

Another muttered, "I'm going home. The people, the noise, the sights! I'm tired!"

My cousin's husband, Peter, who literally jumped over barbed wire into West Berlin in 1961, was skeptical. "The same people are still in power. I don't trust them."

Neither East nor West Berliners felt reunification important. East Germans want to build up the country's economy, their standard of living, and hope to be able to join the European community as equals.

To the East of The Wall

On a bright, calm Sunday my sister and I explored East Berlin where I hadn't been since 1960. East Berlin was a ghost town. No color, people or sound. Everyone was in the West.

East Berlin is a treasure chest of old architecture, bridges, museums, and churches, dating as far back as 1230 AD. Knowing that I wasn't surrounded by repression made a visit East enjoyable for the first time in my life. We touristed until dark. Many times we walked in the center of the street for a better look at the facades of buildings. It was wonderful.

We finished the day in *Ermeler Haus*, a restaurant in a restored building overlooking the Spree River. As one of only two occupied tables, we took our time eating and drinking away the mandatory exchange money in 1760s splendor. (One cannot go into East Germany without exchanging valuable 25 West German Mark for almost worthless East Marks and it had to be spent there).

Tearing Down The Wall

Back in West Berlin, I wanted a piece of the Wall and found I was not alone! More crowds. Everybody tried to pry a piece off this structure with anything from nail files to jackhammers. It sounded like a stone quarry. Berliners nick-named them Wall peckers.

Police, patrolling in pairs, often turned strangers into a brotherhood of conspirators. East Germany lodged a complaint against Wall peckers. One West Berlin officer approached a young man with a wink, "I'm giving you a warning that you are destroying public property and could be arrested."

Chipping away at The Wall

Our tools quickly slipped into pockets and knapsacks. When the policemen walked away, we stood around giggling, waiting for them to disappear around the bend. One man followed to the corner, gave an "all clear," and the chipping continued. The lookout was rewarded with a white and blue graffiti chip.

I attacked the Wall with great satisfaction, equipped with a mason's chisel and hammer. I pounded and pounded until I got my chunk of the Wall to take home and remember.

◆◆◆

Background

"CUT!!!" the director shouted. Everyone stopped on the spot. I was an extra, in the film industry referred to as "Background," on the movie set of *The Cadet Murder*. The TV movie-of-the-week was being filmed at a studio in Wilmington, North Carolina.

As a little girl I wanted to be a movie star. I hadn't seen any movies yet, but heard much talk about revered actors and actresses. My cousin Ingrid and I usually were playing movie star instead of with dolls. I was 10 when I saw my first movie in the neighborhood theater. All the stories were magic; they transported me to distant places. Matinees were mostly comedies, westerns or Esther Williams movies. How we loved Esther! Ingrid and I were forever swimming and diving with a perky smile at the public pool, just like Esther. As I got older my mother put an end to the acting bug, "You need to get a real job."

Love of movies stayed with me. When I came to America in the early sixties, I started watching the Academy Awards every year, rooting for my favorites.

I passed the movie bug onto our daughter. One day, I let her play hookie from junior high so that we could scout out the location where *The Four Seasons,* with Alan Alda, Carol Burnett, Rita Moreno and others, was being filmed. It was a short drive to nearby Stowe. From the description of the surroundings, we located the woodsy area off the main highway.

Sure enough. We saw wide tire tracks in the dirt road. "Movie trucks," we nodded. After about a mile we came to a field filled with large trailers. Most back doors were open. There were truck carrying props, electrical supplies, wood and lots and lots of boxes. Some trailers were the dressing rooms for the actors. Men were busy going back and forth to a house at the edge of the field, carrying stuff that we mostly could not identify.

A group of guys was standing around smoking. We sauntered over. "Are they filming in the house?"

"Oh, they've been at one scene for a while in there. They're gonna have a break soon."

"Is it ok if we wait here?"

"If you stay right where you are, they'll be coming your way going to their trailers."

Andrea and I smiled at each other and, indeed, stayed right at that spot. It couldn't have been more than a half hour when we heard the murmur of conversation coming our way. Around one of the trailers came Carol Burnett. We would have recognized her anywhere; she looked exactly like she did on TV. "You found us!" she said with her trademark smile. She signed both our autograph books and headed to one of the trailers.

Rita Moreno came next. West Side Story was the last movie I had seen her in. That was in the 1960s. This was 1980, she was a tad older, but very beautiful and energetic as she walked towards us. "I'll be delighted to sign your book. Be sure to watch the movie when it comes out." Off she went.

Finally Alan Alda emerged. He looked just as we knew him from M*A*S*H. "Oh no, I don't give autographs." I was disappointed. He really was the main reason we had made this trek. Then, with a slight smile he held out his hand, "I give handshakes instead!" He looked me in the eye and after a firm handshake disappeared into his trailer.

Wow! Alan Alda shook our hand. How cool! We had seen enough, got into the car and drove home, talking nonstop about the setting and Carol, Rita and Alan.

Months later Trent and I saw the movie. I recognized the setting around the house. The scene playing out inside was very dramatic and pivotal to the movie. I realized that we caught the actors when they were in the middle of this dramatic scene. Of course, we had no idea at the time. I chided myself for probably interrupting their thought process. "I'm not going to do that again, I vowed, as exciting as it was."

Whenever a movie was being filmed in Vermont, I lined up to be an extra. No luck.

Trent was offered a sales position at a development on Bald Head Island off the coast of North Carolina. In 1994, we moved to Wilmington. Shortly after settling in I heard that Wilmington had a huge movie studio. Actually, Wilmington was called Hollywood East.

The movie industry discovered Wilmington when Italian producer and director Dino De Laurentiis built the first studio in 1984, incorporating the latest technologies and a large water tank for underwater filming. Now owned by *Screen Gems Studios*, it still is the largest production facility in the U.S. outside of California. The variety of neighborhood settings can be adapted to stand-in for different regions of the country. The coastline offered everything from McMansions to fishing shacks. Within a 15-minute drive inland is the countryside of the deep South. On top of these convenient backgrounds, North Carolina was a non-union state. Production companies could save enormous amounts by not paying union wages.

Someone told me that extras were always needed. Suddenly all my long, buried excitement about acting resurfaced. I was a realtor, but the market was in a slump. Working as an extra could supplement our income.

Fincannons, the largest casting company, had an office in the center of town. I walked into their cramped little office. Two upbeat young women were handling the ever-ringing phone and dealing with the public.

"You want to be an extra? Great! We need lots of people." Wow, that was easy.

Jenny and Cara, the office secretaries, were both angling to get jobs as production assistants. For now, they were in charge of extras. I filled out a form with personal information including height, weight and dress size. I filled out the special talents section with tennis player, runner, coach, etc. Those descriptions are helpful when movie companies need specific background. Jenny took a photo and attached it to the card. "Are you available tomorrow, 6 a.m.?"

"Absolutely."

"Wonderful, I'll make a note of that. Many people don't like these early calls. Come to Forest Hill Drive dressed as a jogger and follow the extras sign."

In the morning the adjacent streets of Forest Hill Drive were lined with large tractor trailers and workers hurrying around - a setting that I remembered from the location of the Alan Alda movie years ago in Vermont. The lighting crew was creating afternoon lighting while dawn still reigned.

The neighborhood scene was for *Empire Records*, a movie with Anthony LaPaglia, Renee Zellweger and Liv Tyler. A production assistant told me, "Your cue to move is "Background." Jog slowly until you hear "Cut." And then go back to the original spot." This was an easy assignment. I jogged down the narrow road lined with Live Oak Trees, every time "Background" was called. When Tom Hanks called "Action," the actors started their conversation. The scene was shot over ten times, but I didn't care. I was happy to be on a movie set!

Trent was just as glad for me with this turn of events. He knew what a movie fan I was. "Good for you! You're going to love it and earn some money to boot." I bought my first cell phone so that the real estate office could reach me.

I made it a point to be available when Jenny or Cara called. I worked steadily, sometimes five or six days a week. Extras pay was a flat $55 for an eight-hour day. As soon as a shoot went just one minute over, overtime fees kicked in. That normally didn't happen on outdoor locations. Street scenes were carefully set and timed. Overtime mostly happened indoors.

For example, for the movie *To Gillian on her 37th Birthday*, starring Michelle Pfeiffer, the company rented a waterfront restaurant on the day they were closed. We were there for 20 hours.

One of the many trailers on location was a large kitchen to feed cast and crew. We lined up after the director and stars like Bill Paxton, John Ritter and Brooke Shields, and were served the same delicious gourmet fare.

I reveled in being part of movie making. I had a front row seat for seeing make-believe in action. And I found out that it didn't take the magic out of movies for me.

Sometimes many hours passed between takes. The background coordinator always let us know, "Relax. You have about an hour 'til the next call." When the weather was iffy during outdoor filming, it often turned into a long wait. That only was a challenge when we had to sit on a beach in forty degree temperatures. We waited bundled up in parkas and blankets. When the sun came out again, we continued the beach scene on a make-believe hot summer day.

My new friend, Martha, and I often were in the same productions. Being short, we could easily blend into any background. We watched all scenes when we were not needed. Just in case we were ever called to step out of the background crowd, we decided to take acting lessons.

Wilmington was saturated with acting schools and agents. First, Martha and I took 'acting for the camera.' Where to look, how to move your head, what pace to stride at, were some of the eye-opening sessions. Even when watching, we couldn't tell that actors moved a bit slower than in real life. The camera accelerates all movement.

Typical formal headshot

After that we joined theater classes, participated in many acting showcases and signed up with an agent. We had professional headshots taken which were needed for auditions. The agent made a living when his actors were working. He got us many auditions, work in commercials, even a three-week stint in *Eddie*, a movie with Whoopie Goldberg. No speaking parts yet, however.

It only took three words to be eligible for membership in the Screen Actors Guild (SAG). If we could get the most coveted SAG card, it meant more work and higher pay. Wouldn't that be great!

Derek moved to Wilmington a couple years after graduating from Prescott College. He also had the acting bug. He worked as an extra and was making the rounds of auditions. We met on many sets and worked in all kind of scenes together. Several times we were cast as a couple; we laughed about that!

It often takes hundreds of people to create one scene in addition to actors and extras. Street scenes and large party settings were the most involved. Crews were constantly rearranging sets and lighting. The only time all was quiet was during actual filming. The shooting schedule was tightly arranged to save time and money. Everyone was more relaxed on smaller sets.

After several months as a reliable extra, I was getting more work when only a few of us were needed. I loved those settings where I could really watch up close. As extras we had to absolutely stick to the rules: "Don't make eye contact or talk to the principals."

But principal actors often mingled with us between takes on small sets. The only actor who didn't was Andy Griffith. On the set of the TV-series *Matlock,* an extra was kicked off the set for saying "Hello" to him

The Rose Garden, starring Mary Tyler Moore, Linda Lavin and Dave Winfield, was filmed in many locations around town. I was called to be a nurse in a hospital scene, the lone extra. I changed into the provided nurse's uniform. Make-up was next and I stepped into the trailer. The award winning actors, with make-up bibs covering their outfits, were occupying three of the four seats in front of the brightly lit wall-to-wall mirror. I wanted to leave and wait outside. "No, no, take a seat," Linda Lavin said.

I took the empty one between her and Dave. While my hair and make-up were fussed with, I looked straight ahead. I could see the three of them in the mirror without moving my head. Their banter was about food, "Oh, I love fresh crabs. This area is the best for fresh seafood!" I pinched myself.

American Gothic, starring Gary Cole, was a TV series with a die-hard following. I was a regular on many episodes in a variety of characters from traffic cop to haughty socialite. No speaking parts though; they eluded me so far.

Headshot wearing my tweed jacket

In *The Cadet Murder*, I was a featured extra. As teacher in a lab class that would be interrupted by a couple of girls entering, I was to make eye contact, nod, search for a particular student and motion for him to step up. I wore one of my tweed jackets and a skirt for a professional look.

The actors were young, barely 20, and interacting with extras all the time. "Oh, you need a SAG card. You'll get lots of work with it," David Lipper, who played the teenage murderer, said. The other actors standing around were nodding.

"We'll help you!" Joanna and Holly chimed in, "Here's what you do. Say "Hello! Who are you looking for?" and then motion to David." Sounded doable.

We took our assigned places. The director said "Background! Aaaaaand "Action!"

I was facing the classroom, and all students were bent over their experiments. The classroom door opened and Joanna and Holly entered. I turned towards them and said, "Hello." - "CUT!!!" instantly followed.

"You guys know better than that!" the director yelled. "Stop it. It's not going to work." Apparently this trio of actors had been trying to be helpful to extras throughout the filming.

We were told to go "Back to one," meaning go back to our original positions. I stuck to the director's instructions. We were done after one take.

Weeks later, Trent was playing in an evening ice hockey game and I was flipping through TV channels. I stopped when I saw a familiar setting. A new scene opened and I recognized the back of the tweed jacket I wore as the Cadet Murder teacher. Then my face filled the screen. Wow! I was staring at the television. I had no inkling of the close-up. As the scene unfolded the eye contact clicked, I motioned to Dave to step up, and the three left the room.

I was jumping up and down yelling, "I did it! I did it! I did it!" to no one in particular.

I never achieved SAG status but, out of the background, I had my close-up!

◆◆◆

Marathon

"This is the marathon route we're driving on," our son Derek casually mentioned while he was giving Trent and me the grand tour of Minneapolis.

Marathon! Running a marathon has been on my "bucket list" for years. Actually, I had already given up on the idea.

We were visiting Derek and his family in January 2001, a couple of weeks after my mother, known as Oma in the family, died. Our children, Jake, Andrea and Derek, could not attend her funeral in Berlin. We were planning our own memorial with Derek.

Trent and Derek had very specific memories of my mother from the summers she spent with us in Vermont: Oma handpicking bugs in the potato patch; Oma going for a long walk on the quiet back road, returning laden with elderberries. The wine we made with those berries was undrinkable at first, but after 20 years matured to a very good one. A very vivid memory.

I had my own memories: the stories she recalled about mushroom hunting for much-needed food during the Second World War; her recollections of evacuations and traveling with two small children, my sister and me, at the end of the war; her unabashed love of all foods.

Girls were not encouraged to participate in athletics when I was growing up in Berlin. Later I dabbled with tennis and skiing. Tennis did not capture my interest. Skiing did, but the sport was limited to a few winter months.

Running became my sport by default when I was in my late 30s. It started when Jason joined the cross-country running team in junior high.   Soon Trent and Jason went on evening runs before dinner. I didn't just want to wait in the kitchen. I began jogging also after coming home from my retail store.   Dinner just had to wait.

I laced up my sneakers and started jogging. It was hard and I finished each run with, "I quit!" But I went out again the following evening.

By 1978, I started to love my runs. I switched from running in the evening to going out first thing in the morning. Whether it was 10 below zero or storming, if the roads were at all passable, I was running.

Runner's World magazine became my source for running and training information and I eagerly awaited every monthly issue. Many experienced runners shared tips. The most valuable ones came from Australian Derek Clayton, former marathon world record holder, and Joan Benoit Samuelson, American Olympic Marathon gold medalist.

"Don't waste energy with sideways motions. Run forward and mostly move from the hips down." Derek's quote totally made sense to me. Joan's training tip, "Don't cheat yourself by writing '4 miles' in your training log when you really only covered 3. It adds up and you cannot expect results as if you really did your full training runs." That was sound advice and I focused on quality in my training.

During the ensuing years I targeted certain races as rewards. Every fall Avon sponsored a 4-mile race for women in Central Park in New York City. It became my motivation to tackle the hills I faced no matter which direction I took. I made a training schedule to improve my running times. I flew to many races in New York. I arranged business appointments, went to a Broadway show or the opera, or both, and then lined up to race on a Saturday morning.

One great aspect of this sport is that runners compete in age groups. I actually was looking forward to birthdays and getting closer to the next age level. I liked my training runs in the quiet countryside much more than the noise and competitiveness during races. But I entered a few every year.

Running turned into a family sport. Andrea and Derek also started running and later joined teams in junior high and high school. We entered many races together, competing within our age groups. Those outings were a wonderful time spent together.

After 5 and 10Ks I ventured to 8 and 10–mile races and eventually the half-marathon. A marathon, 26.2 miles, was on my mind's horizon. After ten years of running I felt that I could tackle the distance, but I couldn't find a race that I wanted to enter. Reading course descriptions, I cringed at "rolling hills" or "uphill finish." I also wanted to avoid heat and humidity.

In the mid 90s we moved from the cool temperatures and hilly terrain of Vermont to the heat, humidity and flat land of coastal North Carolina. I found that heat and humidity weren't that bad, increased my training mileage and kept a lookout for a marathon.

Back at Derek's house after the grand tour of Minneapolis in 2001, I immediately searched the internet for marathon information. The course looked mostly flat and was in the fall, my favorite running season. The Twin Cities Marathon winds through Minneapolis and St.Paul. Many turns would make it an interesting course.

I had found "my" marathon.

The race date of October 7 provided ample time to prepare. Being well trained had paid off over these 20 plus years of running. I never had a running injury. I increased my weekly long run throughout the hot summer months, peaking at 18 miles.

Race day in Minneapolis dawned in the high 20s and calm. Starting time was 8 a.m. in the center of town. Derek dropped me off near the starting line. My moral support team, Derek and Suzanne and grandson Dylan, planned to follow the race route by car and catch me near every other mile marker.

Over 8,000 runners set off. The jammed crowd at the starting line quickly turned into a long line of runners bent on finishing.

I felt very good, sticking to the pace I set for myself. People lined the roads cheering. "Go pink jacket!" "Looking good 1986!"

I kept looking for my support team at every mile marker – no familiar faces. Finally at mile 19, just before a steep hill, I heard "Yeah, Heidi, keep going!" My crew was jumping up and down, waving wildly. What a sight! They ran along with me to the top of the hill. "OK. Enough!"

#1986

Derek said. "We're going for an early lunch. See you at the finish!"

That encounter gave me a big boost of energy. I picked up the pace. Only six miles to go. I was enjoying the experience and felt strong. Maybe I'll run another marathon.

But after mile 21, a sharp pain started to go from my right knee to the hip. This never happened before. I had to stop. I thought I might have to quit the race. Quit the race?!? Other runners had been dropping out during the last couple of miles, but I didn't want to.

Out of nowhere I heard my mother's voice recalling an evacuation in Czechoslovakia in 1945. "I carried Margot on one arm while pushing a baby carriage, that had just lost one of its four wheels, with the other. People tried helping to get the wheel back on. It was useless. You were walking along holding on to my coat." The carriage contained all the belongings she was allowed to take. She had to reach a train station five miles away.

My mother didn't have the option of stopping. It took a long time, but she covered the distance. I was determined to do the same. What is pain if that was all I had to deal with?

I focused on my mother and limped along. I tried different strides, stopped to massage my leg, and experimented with running on opposite sides of the road to benefit from the change in camber. Slowly the pain subsided. I counted down the miles.

A mile from the finish I could jog again. With about a quarter mile to go I heard, "Heidi! You did it!" My family was waiting. It dawned on me that after four-and-one- half hours, I was basically there.

At that point I almost didn't make it. Tears were begging to be released, my lower lip quivered uncontrollably and my legs started to wobble. No! I can't fall apart now! Not before I finish!

As soon as I broke the tape, all pain disappeared and elation replaced my shaky emotions. I did it! At the age of 60, my marathon dream had come true. I felt great!

My crew was exhausted.

◆◆◆

Realtor Tales

Getting a real estate license was a logical step after I sold my business in 1984.

Trent had been a realtor since 1968. We always talked about the daily challenges of this business. "The negotiations are going nowhere," he would shake his head "The seller doesn't understand that there are other houses for sale. If he doesn't accept this offer, I'll be showing properties again tomorrow." I became familiar with procedures and terminologies of the real estate business.

When I had my license, Trent was involved with a new home development in Burlington and could use me right away. I immersed myself in all aspects of the neighborhood and worked part-time as receptionist and greeter. Buyer traffic was very slow during the week. The real estate business was not the least challenging. Actually, I found it boring.

I didn't fully embrace being a real estate agent until we moved to Wilmington on the coast of North Carolina. Trent was with new developments again. I worked as general residential broker at the same company. Our home was important to me and finding the right one for families became my specialty.

Generally the showing and buying process did not take long. Researching new listings was a daily priority for me. I needed to be familiar with locations and noteworthy particulars to do my job well. During preliminary phone calls and meetings, I asked clients enough questions to learn about their needs and habits. My intuition would take over and I quickly knew which areas and houses would be a good fit. My buyers found their home by the third or fourth stop. I loved going to work every day.

To stay in touch, I mailed a quarterly newsletter *News You Can Use* to all clients. I included maintenance tips from a home inspector, an easy dinner recipe and a cartoon. When they needed a broker, I was the one they remembered. The newsletter also generated referrals, a much-needed perk in any business.

Many clients, especially families, became repeat buyers and sellers. For example, when Rob and Tracey Fish bought a small home, I was their agent. A couple years later, proud parents of two children, they bought one with more bedrooms. When they wanted to move to a preferred school district, Rob called again, "Heidi, are you free this weekend? We need to look at homes and sell our house as well."

Continuing education was a must to stay current with legal changes and advances in technology. Contracts and agreements were just a couple of pages in days gone by. When Trent became a realtor in 1968, contracts consisted of one page, if at all. A handshake sealed many deals. More than 40 years later, agreements, disclosures and addendums consisted of 25 to 30 pages. With counter-offers, home inspections, repair requests, etc., paperwork easily reached 150 pages or more, each needing to be initialed or signed.

Communications evolved also. In the early days of my career, contact with clients was by letters, fax and telephone. I had to be in the office at all times, preferably glued to my desk, so that I wouldn't miss any calls. Then the pager came along and created a bit more freedom. The receptionist would activate the pager if I had a call. Finally cell phones revolutionized business practices. My office phone was programmed to forward calls to the mobile one. I could be sitting at the beach and my clients wouldn't know the difference.

Electronic lockboxes, attached to front doors hiding a house key, simplified the day-to-day routines. No longer did I have to drive to offices all over town to pick up keys – and later return them.

The internet completely changed the business. Suddenly people could find homes online. They read of super buys people got daily. Buying no longer was about a home. People wanted deals.

I accommodated most requests, except showing properties after dark. The daytime could be dangerous enough. One time I made an appointment to show a home that was rented. "You're all set," the agent told me, "I'll let the tenant know."

On a Sunday afternoon I rang the doorbell, just in case someone was home. No lights were on in the two-story, gloomy-looking house. Just as I flipped a light switch in the hallway, we heard a commotion upstairs. Suddenly a door opened and I saw a shotgun pointing down the stairs, "Get out!" a man yelled. My client wanted to step forward. I put my arm out to hold him back as I looked up at a bearded man clad only in skivvies.

"Didn't you get a call about this appointment?"

"No! Now, get out!"

We did. My whole body was shaking when I calmly apologized to my client who shook his head, "I don't believe what I just saw!" We did start to chuckle with relief as I drove to our next appointment.

Another time, a friend listed one of her properties with me. "I'm selling the big house. Jim and I are divorcing," Mary announced. "Sarah and I already moved back into the one near my mother's." I arranged for the agents in my office to preview her secluded home in the country. "Oh, sure, go ahead, nobody is there," Mary said.

Twenty-five of us caravanned to the house one morning. I noticed Mary's and another car in the garage. After unlocking the door I shouted, "Anybody home?" We were walking down a hallway when I heard a door opening. Mary slowly stepped out of a bedroom, clutching a blanket in front of her naked body with one hand and holding a pistol in the other. She looked dazed.

"Mary! Are you all right?"

She nodded. "Oh...I forgot you were coming."

A muzzle appeared at the doorway, followed by the rest of the gun gripped by her naked husband. Jim looked at us and lowered the gun. "It's not what you think," he said, "I'm just leaving."

"What is going on?" I thought. I wanted to hug Mary but didn't dare. My colleagues and I slowly retreated. Once in the foyer we scrambled out the door. I yelled to Mary, "Call me!"

"Shouldn't we do something?" one man asked outside.

"What can we do? She indicated she's ok," said a woman.

I wanted to hover in the area to see if Jim was really leaving. "Ok, let's give him a few minutes. If he doesn't show, we'll call the police."

We parked our cars along the dirt road just beyond Mary's driveway. Jim left 15 minutes later. Mandy, in my car joked, "Ok Heidi, next time show us a new listing without any drama!"

Mary explained later, "Jim called and wanted to see Sarah. So we drove out and had a congenial evening. It got late. Sarah went to bed. I called my Mom to come and take her to school in the morning. We started drinking. After we finished a bottle of vodka, he wanted sex. When I said "No," he got the gun from the safe and forced me. I had just gotten the pistol hidden in the bathroom when you came. There was not going to be another time."

"Mary! You need to notify the police," I said.

"No, I don't want Sarah exposed to our mess."

"Well, then at least get a restraining order."

She did. She also bought a cell phone so that she could speed dial the police should Jim violate the order.

Not all client relationships stayed congenial. I was the agent for Janet and Paul Bryant as they bought and sold several houses, spanning eight years. In 2004, Janet called, "Heidi, we want to buy a home with a boat slip."

They instantly liked a house under construction in a new neighborhood almost directly on the Intracoastal Waterway. It was at the edge of marshland overlooking the waterway and ocean beyond. We met with the builder and they made an offer that included extensive changes that Janet insisted on. He promised to finish construction as fast as possible. Janet was gushing, "Oh, thank you again, Heidi." and turning to her husband, "I can't wait to put the boat in the water, can you Paul?" The closing couldn't come fast enough for them.

Two weeks later, after a stormy weekend, Janet called extremely agitated, "Heidi, we drove out to the house. It was very windy and we could see waves on the marsh. Why did you even show us such an unsafe property? You should know better. We can't live in a house like that! We want our deposit back."

I was stunned but accepted their wishes and called the builder. He was surprised as well at this wimpy excuse for not buying the house, "Waves huh?! They are boating people!" He continued, "We both know something else is bugging her. They can have their money back."

From that day on Janet called at all hours, "I want to see a house, be there in 30 minutes." She always brought a friend along, another realtor, as if she needed a witness. She clearly tried to create a reason for voiding our buyer's contract and let her friend take over. I was determined not to let that happen.

Because the public perception of realtors is that we are about as trustworthy as a used car salesman, my professional and ethical standards were high. I knew time was better spent paying attention to detail than apologizing. This transaction wasn't any different.

Janet liked a house with a boat slip in an older neighborhood. She looked at it a second time with Paul. They made an offer that was accepted immediately.

It was a long six weeks to the closing. Janet called daily, "I'm driving to the house. I want to measure the rooms again" – or "I need to see the appliances." Her southern-hospitality manners were non-existent. The house was vacant and my office nearby. I could easily accommodate her whims. No matter how rude her tone, I carefully phrased my answers to her pointed questions. I was emotionally exhausted after each meeting. "I've had it! When this is done, I'm quitting," I said to Trent.

"No you won't. You love what you're doing and you're good it. Don't let one unhappy and rude person sway you!"

Finally the closing arrived and went surprisingly smooth, with no last minute demands. I deleted the Bryants from my mailing list immediately.

Over a year later, a major hurricane roared through Wilmington. Trent and I lived in the center of town where the damage consisted of defoliated trees. Being without power and running water afterwards were our biggest challenges. The coastline usually has the most damage. Newspapers and television covered the aftermath in detail.

In the neighborhood where the Bryants almost bought, a few broken off tree branches were the extent of damages. Houses were built to updated construction codes. The adjacent marsh land provided unobstructed runoff.

Janet and Paul's neighborhood was a disaster. Siding was ripped off all houses and scattered throughout. Water had nowhere to disperse and rose quickly in the canals. Boats were piled on top of each other in the yards; some were resting in the live oak trees after the water receded. Although elevated on stilts, the Bryants house was completely flooded.

I didn't quit real estate as I had threatened. When we moved to Taos, New Mexico, I kept going. It was really an ideal way to get to know a new area and its people.

Anything outside the center of town was a challenge unlike any other I had experienced. The majority of dirt roads did not have street signs. House numbers were also nonexistent. The accuracy of directions depended on how many driveways and trees were available as landmarks. "Turn left after the second large willow, go 300 yards, turn left again, after a wooden fence on the right, turn into the second driveway on the left. The house has a dark red door," were typical instructions.

In a short time, I had been on many back roads that natives didn't know existed. In the span of two months, I put more miles on my car than I had in Wilmington in a year.

Buyers and sellers were the same as everywhere else. I had a call from a woman in California. Her dad, one of our neighbors, died and she inherited his property. "My dad spoke highly of you. I want you to sell the house. I want to clear $180,000."

Wow! Definitely California prices! A review of market value showed that $80,000 would be a generous sales price. The property was in a good area but the house needed to be either razed or completely gutted. I mailed all documentation and called Laura. "No way!" she said.

"If you insist I could list it for $100K, but if you want to sell it you should really be closer to $80K," I said.

"Well, you're obviously not qualified. You don't know what you're talking about!"

Another company listed the property for $150,000. Four years later it sold for $60,000.

The real estate market hit bottom in 2010. It looked like it would take a while to recover. I decided that it was the perfect time to retire. I happily left buyers and sellers behind.

◆◆◆

More Forks

———————•—•———————

Painting and writing became more prominent in my life when we moved to Taos in 2007. I had been multi-tasking as far back as I can remember. So, juggling several jobs and major hobbies felt very comfortable.

Just weeks after having settled in, Trent and I met Richard Alan Nichols, called Rich by everyone, gallery owner, artist and, as it turned out, an excellent teacher. I had taken weekly oil painting classes in Wilmington and was ready to continue. I joined Rich's painting class.

Weeks after the painting sessions started, I noticed an advertisement for a 'Memoir Workshop.' The timing was perfect. I was getting to know the area as a realtor, established a painting routine, and had some extra time. Writing is one of my passions.

After selling Heidi of Vermont in 1984, I registered for a journalism course at the University of Vermont in Burlington. I had been devouring the daily newspaper since I could read. Current events always were most interesting to me. I was excited to be learning about journalism.

I found that journalism was not what I imagined. It was now about slanting and opinions, not straight reporting. I was disappointed and reluctantly decided not to pursue that venue.

I became a member of the Vermont League of Writers and was inspired to just write and better my English vocabulary. One of Ann Morrow Lindbergh's daughters, Reeve Lindbergh, also was member of this no frills, focused writer's league. I enjoyed listening to her writings, after having met her mother when I was working in New York. I joined a small writing group and was looking forward to the weekly meetings. I wrote essays about traveling, running and current events. I submitted many pieces to magazines and newspapers and have the rejection notices to prove it.

Some of my letters and essays did get published: Runner's World, The New York Times, and USAToday are among those publications.

After the collapse of the Berlin Wall, I flew immediately to my hometown. The Times Argus in Montpelier, Vermont, published my full-page report of those exciting days that I was able to witness.

I started writing about my German family's history as it is certainly different from Trent's. Our children often asked about my childhood years after World War II in Berlin. Every time I visited family, I verified more and more information. In the ensuing years I accumulated a good number of stories. The all-day memoir workshop in Taos was the start of finally gathering all the information into a book for my family.

Lisa Sharp and Sally Ooms were also at the workshop and eventually became good friends. At the end of that day, Lisa asked, "Are you interested in forming a writing group?" From my previous group experience I knew how valuable the support of other writers can be.

"Yes, definitely," I said.

It took most of a year until we had a solid group. In our weekly sessions we gave and received constructive input. Reading my stories to the group was the first exposure to the public. Their feedback let me know what areas I had to expand and improve. People joined and left; it wasn't for everyone. Finally we jelled into a cohesive group of five.

Our meetings lasted from two to three hours, depending on the work we had to do. Yes, we worked to make the most of this time we set aside each week. My portfolio of stories grew with every week.

Meanwhile I made sure that I also had time for painting. Rich was very inspiring and made learning and growing fun. I started working part-time at Rich's gallery while also continuing my realtor position at Prudential Taos Real Estate. It was easy to schedule my gallery time around appointments.

I met many good artists and was exposed to another business world. Art sales are not an exact science. Some collectors and buyers do want to deal and some artist will be open to it and others are categorically opposed. There is also the chance of fraud, but I never came across that dark underbelly of the art market.

I became a member of a co-op art gallery near the Blumenschein Museum in Taos. As a member I took my turn keeping the doors open. I had never imagined that my art would be in a gallery. It was very exciting when I sold a painting. Even more so when it happened to be one of mine.

Painting New Mexico's landscape

The idea emerged that I should publish my essays about World War II, family history and growing up in Berlin. "You should publish your story. This will be interesting to many people," was the unanimous voice of the writing group. "You're letting people take a peek into the life of an ordinary German family at a challenging time in history - many things we never heard before and couldn't imagine."

I began to think, "Why not publish?" The thought turned into a plan. Writing and editing took on new meanings. I reworked the stories again and again.

Having been involved and associated with writers for years, I knew that finding an agent or publisher could take years. Since I was almost 70, I was not even going to try that very time-consuming option. I decided to take the self-publishing route. A friend from my Vermont writing days turned out to be the venue. Judith Van Gieson, established mystery writer and now also owner of a small publishing house, living in Albuquerque, agreed to be the publisher.

Once that decision was made, the real work began. When I thought I finished the stories, I edited all pages - taking out or adding sentences and paragraphs. Then I mailed the manuscript of 300 plus pages to a line editor.

I found a designer to help with the book cover right in Taos. I wanted a family photo as cover. Leslie helped with the color and placement. She also had the software to get all the specifications from the printing company correct.

After the editor returned the manuscript, I went to work to make the corrections throughout the stories. While immersed in making corrections, I continually made changes as I noticed a need or had a new idea.

If this sounds time-consuming, it was. Luckily by this time I had retired as realtor and could devote all the hours needed to finish the manuscript. When the editing process seemed overwhelming, I took a break and focused on painting. I found that painting completely refreshed my mind and soon I was ready to tackle editing again.

Changes needed to be made constantly. I shepherded my manuscript from publisher, to printer and back to me multiple times. Computers and the internet played a large part in making the process easier. Part of several of our short vacations was spent making corrections and sending the manuscript back once more.

Then finally, one day in early November 2011, I held a proof from the printer in my hands. *After The Bombs – My Berlin* by Heidemarie Sieg (my maiden name) was born. I was so happy, and tears welled up spontaneously. I cried. It took a while to sink in that the book was actually finished.

The dedication to meet weekly proved productive for the entire group. Four of the five regulars, including myself, have a book published. We celebrated every time we held another one's published volume in our hands.

It was only natural that I continued to write. My first book ended when I decided to come to the United States. I had more stories to tell. Some were easier to write about than others. When I needed to step away from the keyboards, I turned to painting again or I cooked up a feast in my large kitchen.

As is documented in this book, cooking is one of my passions, but a cookbook was not in my plans. It evolved while writing this book.

Recipes begged to be included. I decided to collect all my proven recipes, accumulated food knowledge and organize them into a book. Testing and editing recipes kept me busy for over two years. *Why Add Water When Wine Will Do* was published in December 2014.

Finally, I could focus on *Forks in the Road* completely.

◆◆◆

Looking Back

Not all forks in the road turned out to be smooth.

The indoor ice arena project comes to mind. In 1984, after I sold Heidi of Vermont and still a deeply involved hockey mom, I thought I could pull off creating an indoor skating facility in Waitsfield. There was a need. I made a plan of what would it would take; consulted with active members of *The Friends of Harwood Hockey* and went to work.

I called across the country for specs and estimates of funds needed to construct a viable, enclosed arena. Many people were helpful, others not so. A Waitsfield land-owner pledged a parcel in town. Architects, builders and suppliers were positive but non-committal.

After two years of following up on lead after lead, fundraising and publicity, I had a long list of maybe's. Then, two of the "hockey fathers" asked about the progress I was making. "That sounds very promising. Why don't you give us your files and we'll see what we can do."

"Great," I said. "Three are better than one."

"No, no, you're a woman. The two of us will take over," said one of them. I was shocked by their attitude.

This project never materialized.

Twenty years later, an indoor skating facility was built in nearby Waterbury – headed by two women. A postcard from one of the hockey moms in Vermont arrived, "You were simply ahead of the times."

Did I ever get to San Francisco? Indeed I did. In 1987, I finally visited the city on the bay. I felt at home immediately.

I'll never forget a walk over the San Francisco Bay Bridge. Standing in the center of the span, the bridge moving ever so slightly, I was reminded of a day in the Swiss Alps in 1961. I had hiked to the peak of Piz Nair. Overlooking St. Moritz and the mountains beyond, I felt overwhelmingly small. In San Francisco, facing the expanse of the Pacific from the bridge, I realized again that we humans are a minute, fleeting spec in the Universe. That has kept life in perspective for me, especially when I encountered a few bumps along the roads.

What is next?

I don't know, but I will always take a fork in the road when it appears.

Heidi Smith
Taos, New Mexico
2015

Credits

Cover Design: Emily Wilde
Copy Editing: Helen Richardson
Photo on page 51: Malcolm Reiss

All other photographs are property
of the author.

Recipes are copied from
Why Add Water When Wine Will Do
by Heidi Smith

About the Author

*Heidi Smith lives in Taos, New Mexico.
Besides growing as writer, Heidi is a busy master
gardener, prolific oil painter, expert hiker and
still loves to cook.*